CHINUA ACHEBE
Moulded and Shaped Literary Identity of Africa

CHINUA ACHEBE
Moulded and Shaped Literary Identity of Africa

Neeta Pandey

AUTHORSPRESS
Publishers of Scholarly Books

Worldwide Circulation through Authorspress Global Network
First Published 2011
by
Authorspress
E-35/103, Jawahar Park
Laxmi Nagar, Delhi-110 092
e-mail: authorspress@yahoo.com

Chinua Achebe: Moulded and Shaped Literary Identity of Africa
ISBN 978-81-7273-568-5

Printed in India at Tarun Offset, Delhi.

I Dedicate this work to my son

'Rishi'

Who put up with me while I wrote it.

Preface

Achebe was born in Eastern Nigeria in 1930. He was raised in the large village of Ogidi, which was close to the Niger River, and was also one of the first centres of Anglican missionary work in Eastern Nigeria. He is one of Africa's most influential and widely published writers. He is often called the father of modern African Literature. He was cited in the London *Sunday Times* as one of the "1,000 Makers of the Twentieth Century" for defining "a modern African Literature that was truly African" and making, "a major contribution to world Literature."

Chinua Achebe is the author, coauthor, or editor of some 17 books, among them are five novels: *Things Fall Apart*, 1958; *No Longer at Ease*, 1960; *Arrow of God*, 1964; *A Man of the People*, 1966; and *Anthills of the Savannah*, 1987. He is the editor of several anthologies, including the essay collections *Morning Yet on Creation Day* and *Hopes and Impediments*, and the collection of poetry *Beware Soul Brother*. His first and best-known postcolonial landmark novel, *Things Fall Apart* (1958) was published at the age of 28, which proved popular not only in Africa but throughout the rest of the world.

Achebe has also won acclaim for *Arrow of God* (1964), which was the winner of the New Statesman—Jock Campbell Award; *Christmas in Biafra* (1973), a joint winner of the First Common Wealth Poetry Prize; and *Anthills of the Savannah* (1987), a finalist for the prestigious 1987 Booker Prize. Achebe has received numerous honours from around the world, including the Honorary Fellowship of the American Academy of Arts and Letters, as well as more than 30 honorary doctorates from universities in England, Scotland, the United States, Canada, Nigeria, and South Africa. He is also the recipient of Nigeria's highest honour for intellectual achievement, the Nigerian National Order of Merit.

Achebe's *Things Fall Apart* which got its title from William Butler Yeats's *Second Coming,* was listed among Africa's best books of the twentieth century. Yeats and T.S. Eliot are among Achebe's most favourite poets. The books of Nobel prize-winners, Wole Soyinka and Naguib Mahfouz, were also amongst the top 12 Africa's books of the twentieth century.

Achebe always believed that the power lies in argumentation and persuasion. In his conversation with *Bill Moyers* he said, "Wherever something stands, something else stands beside it. There is no one way to anything.... If there will be one God, there will be others as well. If there will be one point of view, there will be others as well...." On one hand, he says that Christianity did much damage to the minds of Africans, on the other, he says that he has no hatred for the rulers or the Westerners. He feels that a good storyteller should have no business with politics as they have a different agenda. He expects his colleagues in the west to relax and not worry about the Africans as the African writers are in a better position to describe about their history and culture.

In the past, Achebe's controversial views have put him in danger. The 78-year-old novelist has survived an assassination attempt, and in 1990 a serious road accident left him confined to a wheel chair. But in the past three years, he has made a remarkable recovery, and to the surprise of his family and many friends throughout the world, is beginning to look and sound like his old self.

In an interview on *CNN'S African Voices* he said, "If Africans feel they are the greatest sufferers in the world, they are wrong. A man is banished for life; a man loses all his yams and children. But then a man doesn't commit suicide." He himself had six wives but is left with one. He accepts the hard reality that he buried 22 of his children himself and even his daughter buried many of her twins. But then he says that he did not hang himself. Similarly, Africans should strive hard for bringing about order in their lives instead of falling a prey to circumstances.

Broadcasting in the Nigerian government before joining the Biafran Ministry of Chinua Achebe was baptized Albert Chinualumogu in Ogidi in Eastern Nigeria, on November 16, 1930 and was raised by devout Christian parents, Isaiah Okafo, a churchman and Janet N. Achebe. His parents were early converts to Christianity and travelled for 35 years to different parts of Igboland, spreading the gospel. Chinua's grand-parents were tribals that made Achebe write about the tensions between the Christian religion of his parents and the older religion of his ancestors. He was the fifth of their six children. On *CNN'S African Voices* he concerted, "When I wished to be a novelist, there was no protest from my parents, but there was no rejoicing either. I was lucky to have born in such a family where the members donot impose on others." On going away to the university, he shortened his first name to its present better known form— 'Chinua' — as a tribute to Victorian England. He schooled at Government College, Umuahia before earning a graduate degree from University College, Ibadan.

His achievement, however, has not been limited to his continent but is considered by many to be one of the best novelists now writing in the English language. "The ability to shape and mould English to suit character and event and yet still give the impression of an African story is one of the greatest of Achebe's achievements," says R.Angogo, Busara. Achebe feels that as he has written his novels in English, the whole of the African continent could read the books. And if he would have written in Igbo language, just one of the ethnic groups would have had access to it. He also considers English to be a very powerful weapon as a counter agruement to colonization. His voice is the voice of Ancient and Modern Africa.

Achebe—the scholar, cultural historian and the globally acclaimed writer—has been a significant and binding source for an engaging understanding of African colonial, precolonial, and postcolonial history and realities. Such an insight has made him a favourite of Africans, Americans and other scholars. He has given a better and realistic understanding of Africa, at least from Achebe's utilization of his rich and dynamic Igbo ancestry, in South-Eastern Nigeria. He presents before the readers a complex and sympathetic portrait of a traditional village culture in Africa. He is not only trying to inform the outside world about the rich Igbo culture, but also to remind his own people of their past, and to assert that it contained much of value. His view is that whether its Waugh's, *A Handful of Dust* or Conrad's *Heart of Darkness,* one should read with an open eye. He disagrees with Joyce Cary and

Virginia Woolf who feel that the ideal reader is one who completely gives himself over to the writer. According to Achebe, the real trouble begins here.

After the civil war, Achebe was appointed as Senior Research Fellow at the University of Nigeria, Nsukka, and began lecturing widely abroad. From 1972 to 1976, and again from 1987 to 1988, he was Professor of English at the University of Massachusetts, Amherst, and also for one year at the University of Connecticut, Storrs. He is presently Charles P. Stevenson, Jr. Professor of Languages and Literature at Bard College. He is also Emeritus Professor of English at University of Nigeria, Nsukka, founding editor of the *Heinemann Series on African literature*, (1962), founding editor of *Okike – An African Journal of New Writing* (1971), and founding editor of the *Association of Nigerian Authors* (1981).

Today, Achebe lives with his wife in Annandale-on-Hudson, New York, where they teach at Bard College. They have four children who are all successful, with two recently earning doctorates, a third completing a medical degree, and the fourth attending graduate school at Columbia University. Chinua Achebe can be summed up in one metaphor: the *eagle on the iroko*. Iroko is the tallest strongest tree in the forest and the eagle is, of course, the king of the birds. He has literarily climbed and soared above the iroko several times. His colleague at the Bard College, Bradford Morrow, feels that it is a matter of shame that Achebe—a hero in his native Nigeria and well-known throughout the rest of Africa—remains less appreciated in America. When Bradford interviewed Achebe, he asked indirectly to make him comment on his not being the beneficiary of the Nobel Prize. Achebe answered that if a novel does not in an open way address state politics, the politics of organizing a country or culture, is not less beneficient or of lesser value than a political novel. He feels that a book cannot be disqualified for the reason that it does not deal with politics on the state or world level. He means that in his novels there is a politics of family, of love relationship, of religion and politics of walking across the street. He hopes to create a new and progressive nation. He says, "What we missed out in the 20th again we should not miss out again in the 21st century." He also feels that women should always be in the action all the time so that things remain under control.

Neeta Pandey

Acknowledgements

At the outset, I express my gratitude to Dr. Jaydeep Sarangi, a leading Indian bilingual academic and the Assistant Professor of the Department of English, Jogesh Chandra Chaudhuri College (Calcutta University), Editor, *Seva Bharati Journal of English Studies*, Editor-in-Chief, *Titas*, and Executive Member, IACLALS, with whose support and cooperation this book has been published. His suggestions have added value to my work. Grateful thanks are due to my publishers Authorspress, New Delhi, and especially to the, guiding force Sudarshan Kcherry, for giving a final shape to this literary piece.

I am extremely grateful to Dr. Qamar Talat, Professor Department of English, Govt. V.Y.T.P.G. Autonomous College, Durg, and Dr.A.A. Khan for their motivation and guidance. I owe my indebtedness to Madam M. Perwin Rasheed, Principal, Delhi Public School, Durg, whose confidence in me lent wings to my work.

I am grateful to my husband Rajeev Pandey who has been wonderfully helpful and supportive throughout. My special thanks to my mother Mohini Narula, brother Arun Narula, sister-in-law Sonu Narula, to my aunt Rama Narula and uncle Krishan Narula residing in US, for extending all their help. My father Dharam Bir Narula and my sister Poonam Pahwa have been a source of inspiration for writing this piece of work.

I wish to place on record my thanks to the Libraries of Ravishankar Shukla and Banaras Hindu University for providing critical material relevant to my research work. I am extremely thankful to Raju, Proprietor Hindustan Computers, Bhilai, for his concerted efforts in this regard.

Neeta Pandey

Contents

1 Introduction

Dr Neeta Pandey's book is not definitive; it aims to encourage readers to explore further and discover the rich heritage that exists in Ibo society in relation with *Things Fall Apart*, a novel by the Nigerian author Chinua Achebe. Her book has rightly depicted the Ibo society where men were allowed to marry many times depending on their socio-economic status. It has close affinities with the Islamic culture which also permits a man to marry four times as per his economic background. Though in the past, these marriages were conditional, today in the modern age, this practice is being misused by men.

As is evident, Neeta wears many hats and she maintains the gravity of the problem appropriately. In *Things Fall Apart*, Achebe has presented an androcentric world where the man is at the centre and the woman marginal position. As Leonard A. Podis and Saaka Yakubu note that, "The African male may be seen to occupy simultaneously the role of the oppressed (in relation to the colonial masters) and the oppressor (in relation to the African Women)" ("Watermarks"). Neeta voices about the social reality; Achebe's female characters who are silent, voiceless, and invisible; whose social position is no more than a household object.

In his novels, Achebe has depicted the Ibo society where anything strong is associated with man, and anything weak to woman. The title of the novel has a literary source: from William Butler Yeats's poem "The Second Coming".

Things Fall Apart is a 'staple book' in schools throughout Africa and widely studied and researched in English-speaking countries around the world, from Mexico to Australia and Canada to India. Themes throughout the novel include change in society in the aftermath of colonialism, loneliness, abandonment, fear, and importance of social relationships.

Things Fall Apart has been designated as a modern Greek tragedy. It reminds us the plot matrix of a typical Greek tragedy, including the use of a Tragic Hero after Aristotle. Okonkwo is a tragic hero. He shows multiple traits of a classical tragic hero like 'hamartia', 'hubris' (pride) and 'ate' (rashness), and these tendencies in character lead to his 'peripeteia', or reversal of fortune, and his tragic downfall at the end of the novel. Any society in a whirlpool of change breeds many negative feelings like alienation, anxiety, insecurity, fear etc. Okonkwo is socially distressed, brought up by white men, because he has worked hard to move up in the traditional society. It makes references to many iconic texts of the last century in a thought-provoking exchange of ideas or as a creative engagement with them for eliciting further insights into the nature of human realities. Intersexuality does not impede in the textual process but facilitates the flow of the events and controlling the prevailing ideas behind them. It is a lyrical meditation on literature, culture, politics and philosophy of ideas that has animated human discussions and mental horizons so far.

I find the book extremely reader friendly, and it crackles with joy in living and loving; joy in the vivid and animated, weird, complicated poetics that is ordinary life. While reading I am reminded of the famous Orissan English poet, Bibhu Padhi's lines:

> The small things
> keep happening.
> ('Announcement: Early Morning')

Dr. Pandey's research work is the showcase of elegant craft and it is a signal debut work by a promising Indian critic for whom the entire reading world is a big inviting canvas. This well-researched book pushes the limiting boundaries of acceptance. The form is dynamic, the tone pluralistic. The fresh-look critical book is a good read for those who want intellectual nourishment from a work of serious art in an age where anything serious is suspect in popular imagination.

Jaydeep Sarangi

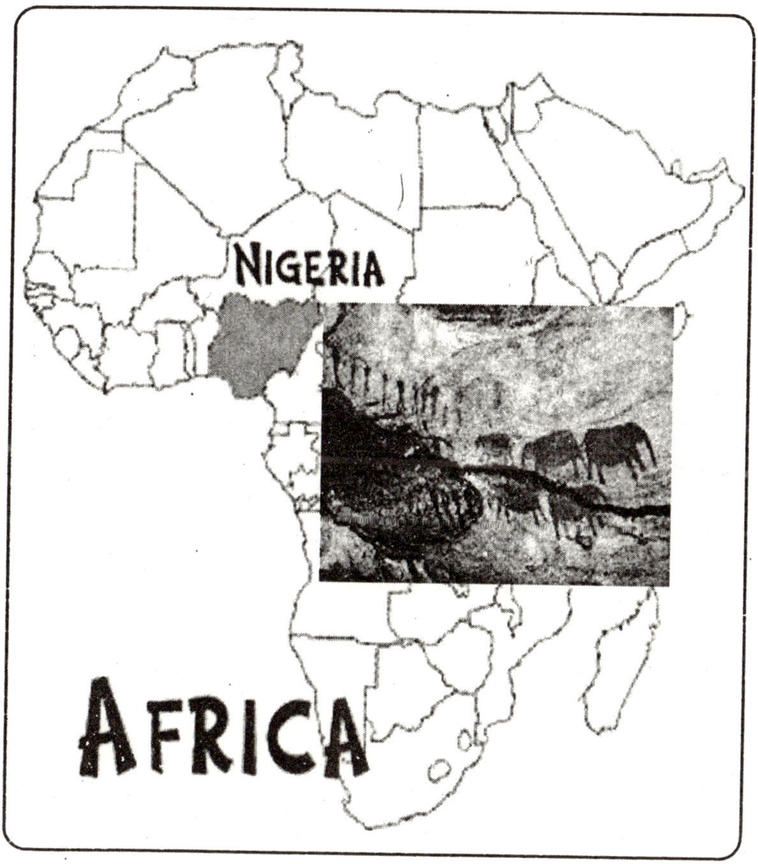

Fig 1. Marq de Villiers and Sheila Hirtle, *Into Africa, San ("Bushman") Paintings* in a shallow cave in the Cedarberg Mountains, not very far from Cape Town (US: Key Porter, 1999).

Africa has a unique cultural heritage with a distinct past. To explore the history of Africa has always remained a mystery. It is not that only Africa has been looted, but even its 'History' has been captured by the white people. The youngest generation in Africa has been made to believe that everything worth has originated from USA. As the African society maintained their culture and tradition verbally, the real history of Africa has been forgotten by the people. Only a few tribes wrote about their life and culture and even these traces have been wiped out by the Europeans. The white people were not willing to believe that the African tribes could build rich civilizations like Zimbabwe before their arrival to the African continent. They even tried to convince the Africans of the prevalence of an old White civilization in the middle of Africa as they claimed to have arrived in Southern Africa at the same time as the black people arrived. But now with the end of cultural imperialism, the history of Africa is being unfurled exhibiting Africa's rich cultural past. This has enabled the youth in Africa to restore pride and faith in their old continent where humans first walked.

It is in Africa where the oldest fossils of the early ancestors have been found. It is through Africa, that Christianity became the religion of the world, and Islam came to play its great role of conqueror and civilizer. Africa came into the Mediterranean world mainly through Greece that had been under African influence. Africa was cut off from the melting pot by the turmoil among the Europeans. Africa prior to these events, had developed its history and civilization, indigenous to its people and lands.

It is in Africa, the "dark continent", that the fossil remains of several species of early ape like humans, thought to have evolved into modern day man, such as Australopithecus, Afarensis, Paranthropus Boisei, and Homo ergaster, has been discovered. During the mid twentieth century, anthropologists found the evidence of human occupation, perhaps as early as 7million years ago. The scientific studies show that Africa, particularly the eastern and the southern regions, are the cradle of human-kind. As per most of the records and the studies made, Africans are one of the oldest people on the face of the earth. And the fact cannot be denied that the people and the culture of Africa are older than the word "Africa". The Africans were the ones who could influence the Greeks and the Romans and also the early world which is known today as Europe. According to the great historian, W.E.B. DuBois:

> Always Africa is giving us something new...On its black bosom arose one of the earliest, if not the earliest, of self-protecting civilizations, and grew so mightily that it still furnishes superlatives to thinking and speaking men. Out of its darker and more remote forest vastness came, if we may credit many recent scientists, the first welding of iron, and we know that agriculture and trade flourished there when Europe was a wilderness ("Why Africana History?").

Christianity and Islam, the alien religions on the land, brought about a great change in Africa. Both the religions compelled the convert to shed their indigenous names, names that narrated their beginnings and conferred on them their individual and historic identities. Conversion to Christianity was basically through military conquest, terror of enslavement, and economic controls. The islamic invaders inaugurated the era of slave raids on the black continent for Arab slave markets: "Islam began the work of destruction. But Europe did a better job" (qtd. in Soyinka, *The Burden of Memory* 52-53). With the Christian missions came literacy, education and hope, and acceptance for the disadvantaged. But it showed no tolerance for people's culture and ceremonies. Unlike Christianity, Islam showed some considerations to their traditional values, like it allowed a man, to have more than one wife. That is the reason why for the Africans the conversion to Islam became easier and less upsetting than conversion to Christianity:

> While every day in the West, roughly 7500 people in effect stop being Christians every day in Africa roughly double that number become Christians (qtd. in Isichei, *A History of Christianity* 1).

Africa, which is the world's second largest and second most populous continent, has over 84 crore people spread in 61 territories, which account for more than 12 per cent of the total world population. Nigeria, whose official name is the Federal Republic of Africa, is by far the most populated of Africa's countries, with more than one-seventh of the continent's people. Lagos, along the coast, is the largest city, and the country's economic and cultural centre. But the government moved from Lagos to Abuja in 1991 in the hope of creating a national capital where none of the country's ethnic groups would be dominant.

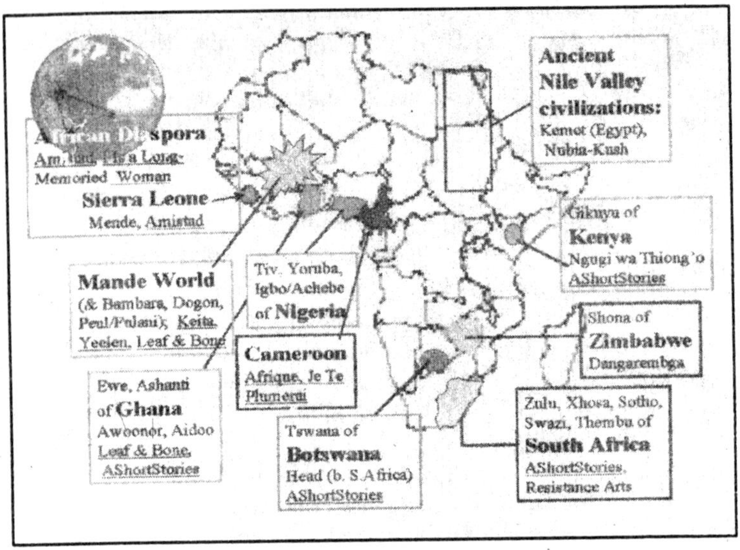

Fig 2. African Diaspora, various ethnic groups

Source: Electronic

The Nigerians belong to different ethnic groups which give the country a rich culture. But it also poses a major challenge to the nation building. Nigeria's three largest ethnic groups—the Hausa-Fulani, Yoruba, and Igbo—represent about 70 per cent of the population. The Igbo inhabit the territory of South-Eastern Nigeria, and their homeland is located on both banks of Orimili [the great river], the River Niger, from which Nigeria derives its name. According to Basden, "the Ibo nation ranks as one of the largest in the whole of Africa" (qtd. in Okpewho, *A case Book* 68). About 10 per cent of the total ethnic population consists of several other groups numbering more than 1 million members each, including the Kanuri, Tiv and Ibibio. More than 300 smaller ethnic groups account for the remaining 20 per cent of the population. William Fagg in his excellent new book, *Nigerian Images,* says:

> ... Nigeria was created by the British— for their own ends. Let us give the devil his due: colonialism in Africa disrupted many things, but it did create big political units where there were small, scattered ones before. Nigeria had hundreds of autonomous communities ranging in size from the vast Fulani Empire founded by Usman dan Fodio in the north to tiny village entities in the east: Today it is one country (Okpewho, *A Case Book* 58).

It was through the Romans that the name 'Africa' came into Western usage who used it as Africa terra, that is, the "Land of the Afri" as plural and 'Afer' as singular. The Afri were basically a tribe known as 'Berber' who resided in North Africa in the Carthage area. The origin of Afer may be connected with Phoenician 'afar'—"dust"; or the latin word 'aprica', meaning "sunny"; or the Greek word 'aphrike' meaning "without cold", which even today is still a debatable issue. The Greeks referred to Africa as "The Land of the Burnt-Face People." Just like all other continents, Africa's prehistory had no nation states and was instead inhabited by groups of hunter-gatherers, such as Khoi and San [formerly known as bushmen].

Around 3300 BC, the historical record opens in Africa with the rise of literacy in Egypt. The River Nile — the world's first cultural highway, offered the Africans bounteous opportunity to build prominent civilizations like the Egyptian, Ethiopia, Kushite, Meroitic, the Kingdoms of Ghana, Mali, Songhai, and great Zimbabwe. The penetration of North Africa, West Africa and Sudan by the Arabs had cemented a rich Swahili culture, that is, a fusion of African and Arab culture. This had led to the marriage between women of Africa and men of the Middle East, and fusion of this had led to the urban and agricultural communities which was rich in architecture, textiles, and food.

African art, music, and occupation reflected the diversity of the African culture. The oldest existing art from Africa are 6,000 year-old carvings found in the Niger. It is the Great Pyramid of

Giza in Egypt which was the world's tallest architectural accomplishment for 4,000 years until the creation of the Eiffel Tower. The music of Africa is one of its most dynamic art forms. The rhythms of Sub-Saharan Africa, in particular West Africa, were transmitted through the Atlantic slave trade to modern blues, jazz, rap, and rock and roll.

Portuguese traders brought the first African slaves for agricultural labour to the Caribbean in the fifteenth century. They set up many of the trading stations along the Guinea coast at Elmina. The trade mainly comprised slaves, gold, ivory, and spices. The first Nigerian slave was Olaudah Equiano or Gustavus Vassa who was sold at the tender age of eleven. Of the white people he observed that: "I had gotton into a world of bad spirits and that they were going to kill me." (qtd. in February, *Mind Your Colour* 34). The European Discovery of America in 1492 further boosted the slave trade which could not remain confined to any one continent:

> The Afrikanners (Devout Calvinists) have always considered themselves the civilising force in the country, having trekked inland by Ox-wagon, carrying a gun in one hand and a Bible in the other (qtd. in Mehta, and Narang, *Apartheid in Fiction* 9).

The earliest Dutch arrivals looked down upon the natives Hottentots and Bushmen but without discrimination. There was not any philosophical problem as such because the natives were very simple and illiterate. They were exploited as per the needs, and some were forcibly converted to Christianity. A vast majority of them were deprived of their possessions; killed like animals or enslaved, and a few were adopted as equals in the white man's civilization. However, there was no prejudice on the basis of colour. Race relations had not been invented in the seventeenth century and apartheid had not yet become a principle. It was merely an exploitation of the weak by the strong. A slave had every opportunity to work hard and attain success and more so after conversion to Christianity:

> When a slave was brought by Smith, that slave was renamed Smith; the same thing was later transferred to the colony. It meant that if an African was baptized, as evidence of his new

> self or the new identity he was given an English name. Not just a biblical, but a biblical and English name (Thiong'o, *Writing Across Worlds* 328).

The first brick of the impenetrable wall of apartheid was laid a century and a half later when the marriages between the white men and the natives was prohibited in 1695, and that wall still exists, and is unbroken today. The Afrikaaners or Dutch pursued a policy of racial segregation to show the superiority of the Europeans. And then different queues, different compartments, and divided archway started playing a significant role, declaring blacks as inferiors and destined for menial jobs. The life of a man of colour in South Africa became intolerable. The blacks were shot, slashed and beaten up by the police:

> A black skin is considered by the Khaki uniformed iron-faced members of the police a sufficient invitation to halt a man in the street, demand any one of a number of documents which are supposed to attach to the living body of an African and on his failing to produce it, to load him on Kwela Kwela or frogmarch him to the nearest police station (qtd. in Mehta, and Narang, *Apartheid in Fiction* 8).

It was not before 1952 that the African National Congress, with assistance of a few whites, started its resistance campaign which aimed to reduce apartheid to lower levels. The tolerance of the Africans is reflected in the patience of the writers, especially in the words of Wole Soyinka who expressed himself in *Writing Across Worlds*:

> A few years ago in a lecture in England I said I was giving apartheid ten more years. A few years later in another lecture I said, 'A few years ago I gave apartheid ten more years. I am afraid something must have happened to me which made me so optimistic' (28).

Europeans, such as Portuguese and Dutch, and American slave traders next ravaged the African continent in the beginning of the sixteenth century. This trade mainly comprised Igbo slaves, one of the most popular ethnic groups in Nigeria. They were spread over an area of 100 miles in South-Eastern Nigeria at the confluence of the Niger and Benue Rivers. African slaves were quite experienced in cultivating rice, cotton, sugar, and all crops grown in West and North Africa. These skills helped Africa in becoming a plantation economy. Other skills possessed by the Africans comprised ironsmithy, music, and musical instruments, the decoration arts and architecture. This enabled them in shaping a hybrid American culture. Until 1860, it is estimated that more than 10 million people were transported from Africa to the America, and a majority to the Caribbeans, Brazil, or the Spanish colonies of Central and South America. The territories that are now Ghana, Togo, Benin, and Nigeria were the origins of most slaves brought to North America, although significant numbers also came from the areas that are now Senegal, Gambia, and Angola. The Europeans loaded the captured Africans onto specially constructed ships with platforms below deck designed to maximize the number of slaves that could be transported. The Africans were confined for two or three months in irons during the crossing of the Atlantic Ocean called the 'Middle Passage'. The slaves were given a meagre diet of rice, yams, or beans. This along with the filthy conditions created by overcrowding resulted in a very high death rate. Many ships reached their destination with barely half their cargo of slaves still alive, to sell into forced labour in America. The first Africans brought to the English colonies in North America came on a Dutch privateer that landed at James town, Virginia, in August 1619. The ship had started with about 100 captives, but as the ship had run into extremely bad weather, it had only 20 surviving Africans to sell to the struggling colony. Soon many of the colonies along the Atlantic seaboard started importing African slaves. The Dutch West India Company brought 11 Africans to its garrison trading post in New Amsterdam [known today as New York City] in 1626, and Pennsylvanians imported 150 Africans in 1684.

The African slaves had been through traumatic experiences, and were forced to make a new life for themselves far from home, in close proximity to people different in languages and culture. They adopted European names and Western dress, and learnt English. As early as the 1700s, the British trade in Africa had shifted entirely to slaves:

> Men in Europe were accustomed to seeing Africans only as men in chains, captives without power, and they transferred their impressions to Africa and the states from which these

> slaves had come. The belief in African inferiority was already in full bloom (qtd. in Achebe *Home and Exile* 28).

A new trading era focusing on the industry [palm product, timber, elephant tusks, and spices], came into existence with the abolition of the slave trade by Britain in 1807. It enlisted other European nations also to enforce the ban. Britain's motivations were partly humanitarian and partly economic. In the words of a visitor to the Gold Coast in the late seventeenth century:

> The great concern of the *Dutch* on this coast, as well as of all other *Europeans* settled or trading there, is the gold, and not the welfare of those souls: for by their lewd loose lives, many who live among these poor wretches rather harden them in their wickedness than turn them from it (qtd. in Isichei, *A History of Christianity* 54).

The British Empire no longer had American colonies whose economic growth depended on slaves, and moreover due to industrialization, Britain needed Africa's raw materials more than its people. Consequently, trade in products such as palm oil, which European valued highly as an industrial lubricant, replaced the trade in humans. And thus the European merchants encouraged the missionaries to send them the samples of dyes, cotton, ginger, pepper, coffee, palm oil, ivory etc. Most of Nigeria's former slave-trading states were weakened by the loss of income. British trading companies such as the United Africa Company took advantage of the weakened empires and established depots at Lagos and in the Niger Delta. Some of the explorers who were funded by the trading companies, laid the groundwork for the eventual expansion inland of the trading companies. Missionaries also facilitated the process of replacing the slave trade with "Christian Commerce" by acquiring real fluency in Igbo. The British Evangelicals tended to believe that:

> ...The development of alternative forms of commerce was the surest way to eliminate the slave trade: 'The mills of Manchester... will yet shout for joy through the cotton wealth of the Niger districts' (qtd. in Isichei, *A History of Christianity* 83).

The first British settlers who were five thousand in number arrived in Africa in 1820. They came as farmers who were basically dependent on agriculture. Unlike the Dutch, they had close links with their country and did not want to be individual pioneers: "They wanted to reproduce a kindlier Britain on the shores of Africa" (qtd. in Mehta, and Narang, *Apartheid in Fiction* 10).

In 1900, the British imposed their administration upon the Igbos by dividing south-eastern Nigeria into areas ruled by District Commissioners, and appointed competent Igbos to act as warrant chiefs, clerks, and messengers to assist them. This attempt by the British to take over political control of Igboland met with resistance and cultural protest in the early decades of the twentieth century. As they were fully confident of their administration and authority, the engine of imperialism could not be stopped. The Igbo culture lost its value and significance, which could never be the same again. While most of Africa had achieved Independence by the early 1960s, southern African colonies took longer to become independent. And it was not until 1994 that South Africa was returned back to her people and governed through majority rule. When Africa got independence in 1960, the impact of colonialism could still be seen on their national anthem:

> So we found ourselves on independence morning rolling our tongues around the very same trickster godling:
>
> Though tribe and tongue may differ
> In brotherhood we stand!
>
> (Achebe, *The Trouble with Nigeria* 6).

In May 1967, when the Lieutenant Colonel, Yakubu Gowon, announced the creation of a new 12-state structure in Nigeria, regional and ethnic tensions escalated quickly which led to the Biafran war—the war between Northern [Nigeria] and Eastern [Biafra] Nigeria. The Eastern Region, populated mostly by Igbo, had to be divided into three states, two of them dominated by non Igbo groups. The division would also separate the vast majority of Igbo from profitable coastal ports and rich oil fields that had recently been discovered in the Niger Delta [which until then was a part of the Eastern Region]. The leaders of the Eastern Region saw this action as an official attempt to push the Igbo to the margins of Nigerian society and politics. On 27 May 1967, the regions' Igbo-dominated assembly authorized Lieutenant Colonel, Odemegwu Ojukwu to declare independence as the Republic of Biafra. Ojukwu obliged three days later. War broke out in July 1967 when Nigerian forces moved south and captured the university town of Nsukka. Biafran troops crossed the Niger River, pushing deep into the west in an attempt to attack Lagos, then the capital. Gowon's forces repelled the invasion, imposed a naval blockade of the south-eastern coast, and mounted a counter-attack into northern Biafra. A bitter war of attrition followed, prolonged by France's military support for the Biafrans. In January 1970, the better-equipped federal forces finally overcame the rebels, whereupon Gowon announced that he would remain in power for six more years to ensure a peaceful transition to democracy. But the Igbo rebuilt their lives with the same courage and determination they had shown in war. The physical and psychological disruption caused by the war in Nigeria, as well as the increasingly unrestrained economic and political corruption, made sustained writing difficult for literary writers.

African literature reflects the cultural traditions, colonial history, and inner conflicts of African people. In the twentieth century, European narratives of Alan Paton, Nadine Gordimer, and Doris Lessing had produced distorted images of African people and their culture. Nadine Gordimer observes in *The Black Interpreters* that:

> Almost any African who has anything to say about the condition of being African, either in the colonial past or in the independent present, is likely to find interested readers, since he or she has information to offer, an inside story or an experience over-documented from the outside, white-side (qtd. in February, *Mind Your Colour* 139).

Chinua Achebe rejects these images and makes an attempt to provide a true portrayal of African indigenous population and European people through specific symbols and myths. There is a lack of critical works on African literature as the European researches could not rightfully interpret African cultural traditions and customs, and it is believed that: "As African literature emerged only in 50s years of the twentieth century, earlier studies of African people were invalid and wrong" (qtd. in "Embodiment in African Literature").

The British colonial system sidelined the African writers who were also writing in English and could not realize the beauty of their own language.William Wordsworth's poem "Daffodils" or Charles Dicken's "London" were more familiar to them than the landscapes outside their own windows. As Caryl Phillips notes in *The European Tribe*(1987), describing his own schooling in 1970s Britain:

> I was never offered a text that had been penned by a black person, or that concerned the lives of black people.... If the teaching of English literature can feed a sense of identity then I, like many of my... contemporaries... was starving (*Writing Across Worlds* 2).

Prominent Igbo writer—Chinua Achebe of Nigeria, provides an accurate picture of the African past and present—of life with all its pains, pleasures, and puzzles. In his novels, he has spoken of his disillusionment and internal strife within the country. Achebe admits that Africa's development has often been an issue of debate for other writers. He accepts the fact that if Africa has to progress, it will have to overcome many hurdles and problems:

> Africa now ... yes, there's disappointment, pain, sorrow. But I say to myself, when was it in the last 500 years that Africa has not been in great pain and sorrow and disappointment? The answer is, very rarely ("Black History").

Achebe's love for his nation is quite prominent in his novels, where he talks about the rich African culture and values. His works retain the freshness and vigour of the indigenous oral tradition. He narrates about the history and the heritage of the African Continent. He has all praise for Igbo society and feels that they can bring about revolution in Nigeria:

> The Igbo people of southeastern Nigeria are more than ten million strong and must be accounted one of the major peoples of Africa. Conventional practice would call them a tribe, but I no longer follow that convention. I call them a nation (Achebe, *Home and Exile* 3-4).

In his novels, Achebe reflects the strong ethos of hard work for which the Igbo people are known, while the egalitarian organization of society encourages one to believe that there is no limit to what one can achieve in life. It is the same ethos of hard work and high self-esteem that Olaudah Equiano, the first Nigerian Slave, refers to in the description of his Igbo people more than two centuries ago:

> Agriculture is our chief employment; and everyone, even the children and women are engaged in it. Thus we are all habituated to labour from our earliest years. Every one contributes something to the common stock; and as we are unacquainted with idleness we have no beggars (qtd. in Okpewho, *A Case Book* 71).

Achebe feels that only the Africans can best describe their own world to the others. The aliens cannot talk about a country whose culture is unknown to them. In his novels, he condemns the talk of the writers about his nation, whose thoughts could not convince him. Even he finds the view of an American reviewer quite unconvincing which he mentions in his novel *Hopes and Impediments*:

> Perhaps no Nigerian at the present state of his culture and ours can tell us what we need to know about that country, in a way that is available to our Understanding...in the way W.H. Hudson made South America real to us or T.E. Lawrence brought Arabia to life (Achebe 26).

Achebe fails to understand as to why they should wait patiently for others to tell them about their own past. He asserts that a man's identity can be assessed by the strangers but those will be mere assumptions. He does not agree to the German Scholar, Janheinz Jahn who thus defines the term "Authentic Africans":

> Only the most highly cultivated person counts as a "real European. " A "real African," on the other hand, lives in the bush ... goes naked ... and tells fairy stories about the crocodile and the elephant. The more primitive, the more really African. But an African who is enlightened and cosmopolitan ... who makes political speeches, or writes novels, no longer counts as a real African (qtd. in Achebe, *Hopes and Impediments* 27).

It was after reading Joyce Cary's much praised *Mister Johnson,* which portrays a comic African, he decided to describe Africa to the world. A description of Achebe's life and works would be incomplete without the name of a great critic, Joseph Conrad. No writer could be expected to have so much patience so as to read Conrad's novel *The Heart of Darkness* in which he has compared the mankind to a beast. Achebe expresses his agitation on reading the Conrad's account of his first encounter with a black man, where he over emphasizes the word 'black'. He infers that the Africans are quite strange and peculiar creatures.

Africa became a tool of criticism in the hands of the missionaries. They basically wrote about the darker side of African society, and sometimes they even misinterpreted what they saw. The corpses which were left by the Igbos in the grove called *ajo afia,* the evil forest, were assumed by the European observers as human sacrifices. For the Europeans, the African colonies became the 'White Man's Grave' as they suffered miserably due to malaria and yellow fever. The adjectives used in the *Winds of Change* to describe the 'Black Continent' aptly highlights the opinion of the Europeans about Africa:

> Anyone who has lived in Africa knows how awesome are her hours of darkness; a stillness of death pervades the sleeping world of humans, yet one is ever aware of the wildlife which silently creeps from cover with the approach of night, and imagination peoples the thick bush with crouching lions and velvet-footed leopards, and every dancing firefly becomes a glowing eye set in the head of some savage beast (41).

V.S. Naipaul and Joyce Cary have criticized Africa to such an extent that Achebe is without words to express his anxiety. It seems to Achebe that they have the absolute power over narration. That is the reason they have taken the liberty to express their strong dislike for the Africans. The fact cannot be denied that both the writers have written much about Africa, but not for the Africans. Naipaul in a 1980 interview with The *New York Times* had said: "I don't count the African readership and I don't think one should. Africa is a land of bush, again, not a very literary land" (qtd. in Achebe, *Home and Exile* 88-89).

Like Achebe, Cary has also shown the colonial impact on African life. Joyce Cary in his novel *Mister Johnson*, has taken Fada as an ordinary town of western Sudan and suggests that the people of Fada, despite their poverty, lived happily but the impact of Western life brought them all their woes and miseries:

> Strangers are still rare in Fada bush and they are received with doubt. This is not surprising, because in Fada history all strangers have brought trouble, war, disease or bad magic (qtd. in Majumdar, *Joyce Cary* 42).

Achebe seems to be quite tolerant and patient while talking about Joyce Cary's book *Mister Johnson* which was described by *Time Magazine* of October 20, 1952, as "the best novel ever written about Africa." It is quite amazing to see the writers taking undue advantage of their freedom of expresson. Achebe has, no doubt, proved himself to be an 'authentic writer' who does not like to interfere much in the business of others. Who would not be contemptuous of the description given by Mister Johnson about the Nigerians to his friends:

> The demonic appearance of the naked dancers, grinning, shrieking, scowling, or with faces which seemed entirely dislocated, senseless and unhuman, like twisted bags of lard, or burst bladders (qtd. in Achebe, *Home and Exile* 24).

Achebe has much contempt for Cary's novel *Mister Johnson* where he presents an idiotic African as the hero. Mister Johnson is full of emotional vitality and the endearing human warmth of a child. When he is condemned to death, his dearest wish is to be shot death by the European District Officer. And his wish is granted by him. He met with the same treatment as that of horses and cats. Achebe feels the need to present the Africans from their perspective.

Achebe appears to be a great critic as he knows that on one hand, is Africa's breathtaking natural beauty, on the other is Africa's wilderness. He comprehends that his country is not without faults, as there are various problems which it experiences. He does not deny the fact that Africa has to go a long way in order to change its face on earth. This reflects his optimistic thoughts which inspire other writers to reveal the truth about their own country without any bias or prejudice. Achebe admits openly that:

> Nigeria is *not* a great country. It is one of the most disorderly nations in the world. It is one of the most corrupt, insensitive, inefficient places under the sun. It is one of the most expensive countries and one of those that give least value for money. It is dirty, callous, noisy, ostentatious, dishonest and vulgar. In short, it is among the most unpleasant places on earth! (Achebe, *The Trouble with Nigeria* 9-10).

Like Chinua, the Nobel Prize Winner Nigerian Writer, Wole Soyinka, also feels that Africa is not without problems. A number of regimes had to face the problem of corruption and oppression. Every time the Nigerian writer's efforts to talk about the positive aspects of Nigeria goes futile as the view point of the European writers supersedes their own. Soyinka expresses his inability as an individual by saying that:

> We find that we've been frustrated at every turn and we've had to do something like the labour of Sisyphus rolling the stone uphill all the time until it reaches the top, and instead of it being built upon, is given a push back down again. The political forces are such that they have thwarted our attempts.... (*Writing Across Worlds* 27-28).

Ngũgĩ wa Thiong'o in *Decolonising the Mind,* admits that it is the moral duty of the African writers to make the new generation realise the significance of their traditional values. Like Achebe, he also feels that some writers wrongly associate Africa with the negative qualities of backwardness, underdevelopment, and humiliation. Thiong'o strongly asserts that if one wants to comment on the flaws of a nation, one should not forget the positive features of it. That is the reason, he preferred to write in Gikũyũ language, a Kenyan, and an African language to talk of the antiimperialist struggles of Kenyan and African peoples. Thiong'o strongly supports Achebe in his viewpoint that the negative should not be viewed as positive, and the positive not as negative:

> Africa actually enriches Europe: but Africa is made to believe that it needs Europe to rescue it from poverty. Africa's

> natural and human resources continue to develop Europe and America: but Africa is made to feel grateful for aid from the same quarters that still sit on the back of the continent.Africa even produces intellectuals who now rationalise this upside-down way of looking at Africa (*Decolonising the Mind* 28).

Achebe asserts that Nigeria is not beyond redemption, as Africa is always changing and progressing fast. He is quite optimistic about the recognition and the admiration which Nigeria would get from other countries in the future. He is also of the opinion that the Igbos will contribute much to the growth and development of Nigeria as they are dynamic and diligent: "Nigeria without the inventiveness and the dynamism of the Igbo would be a less hopeful place than it is" (Achebe, *The Trouble with Nigeria* 49). Achebe reminds the readers of the moral and the social dimensions which the art has. He accepts that the writers have a moral obligation towards the society who should aim at its reformation. No country should turn its back towards its traditional past as it cannot help the nation in solving its problems. Achebe is of the viewpoint that every nation has something for which it could be admired, and for few things, it could also be criticized. He feels that the expectation of others from Africa is quite high, but they should not expect them to be the angels:

> I would suggest from my privileged position in African and Western cultures some advantages the West might derive from Africa once it rid its mind of old prejudices and began to look at Africa not through a haze of distortions and cheap mystifications but quite simply as a continent of people— not angels, but not rudimentary souls either— just people, often highly gifted people and often strikingly successful in their enterprise with life and society (Achebe, *Hopes and Impediments* 18).

Achebe feels that the African writers should be given their due, as they aim to develop their society. He desires to get rid of the inferiority complex and make them lead a life of self-esteem. He is of the viewpoint that if the African scientists are given an opportunity to provide scientific solutions to the problems of Africa, and if African historians are trusted of their researches, then why the African writers cannot be trusted. This fact is realized by Achebe who hopes to develop confidence and trust in the African writers, as he feels that they can only describe their cultural past. Famous African writers, Wole Soyinka and Ngũgĩ wa Thiong'o, who were denied the right to freedom of speech and expression, are also oı the same opinion. The latter feels that, "it is the fate of Africa to have her destiny always decided around conference tables in the metropolises of the western world" (Thiong'o, *Decolonising the Mind* 4). Another renowned author, Nadine Gordimer also feels the same way. He elaborates further on the question of politics and the problems encountered by the creative writers during the harsh years of apartheid regime.

Achebe's works are a binding source for an engaging understanding of African precolonial, colonial and postcolonial history and realities. He talks of the colonial Nigeria, where the ground work accomplished by the missionaries in the precolonial days is the central concern. Chinua Achebe accepts the fact that Africa has been struggling over the past because of its own mistakes. He even pinpoints towards the root cause of the main problem:

> The trouble with Nigeria is simply and squarely a failure of leadership. There is nothing basically wrong with the Nigerian character. There is nothing wrong with the Nigerian land or climate or water or air or anything else. The Nigerian problem is the unwillingness or inability of its leaders to rise to the responsibility, to the challenge of personal example which are the hallmarks of true leadership (*The Trouble with Nigeria* 1).

After world war II, as African began demanding their independence, more African writers produced poetry, short stories, novels, essays, and plays. In Western Africa, writers like Wole Soyinka, Ousmane Sembene, Kofi Awoonor, Agostinho Neto, Tchicaya u tam'si, Camera Laye, Mongo Beti, Ben Okri, and Ferdinand Oyono; and in Eastern Africa, Ngu~gi~ wa Thiong'o, Okot P' Bitek, and Jacqúes Rabe' Mananjara often shared the same themes. They depicted the clash between indigenous and colonial cultures, condemnation of European subjugation, pride and glory in the African past, and hope for the continents' independent and bright future. In South Africa, the writers like Es'kia Mphahlela, Nadine Gordimer, Bessie Head, Dennis Brutus, J.M.Coetzee, and

Miriam Tlali, reflect in varying degrees the horrors of apartheid, the experience of living in a racially segregated society, which even today dominates literature. Like Ngu~gi~ and Sembene Ousmane, the prominent African writers, who explained and contested the force of neo-colonalism in Africa, Chinua's *Anthills of the Savannah* seems to have a similar preoccupation. Grace Ogot, Buchi Emcheta, Flora Nwapa, Rebecca Njau, Bessie Head, Farida Ksodia, Mariama Ba and other woman writers deal with the impact of neo-colonialism in different ways. Their works assume vital importance in generation of a radical consciousness in the minds of the people.

Among the West African Anglophone writers who endeavour to show a true picture of the African society with its cultural past, its inherent anarchy, its struggle for independence and the disillusioning aftermath of post-independence era, Chinua Achebe is truly outstanding. Achebe was 26 years old when he wrote *Things Fall Apart* and how significant his novel is even in the present-day times. It has been translated into about 40 different world languages and it has sold over 60 million copies. His best and maiden novel *Things Fall Apart*, got its title from W.B. Yeats's poem "The Second Coming". Just as Yeats exhibits the gyres of anarchy in Western civilization due to lack of religious faith, Achebe's novels too describe the degeneration of nature values and culture in Africa. It shows the continual struggle experienced by the Igbos in a world of motion and change which was like a tightrope walk. Achebe admits:

> When my first novel appeared in 1958 with the allusive title *Things Fall Apart*, an offended and highly critical English reviewer in a London Sunday paper titled per piece—cleverly, I must admit--Hurray to Mere Anarchy (*Home and Exile* 18).

Chinua Achebe's *Anthills of the Savannah* and ken Saro-Wiwa's *A Forest of Flowers*, describe all aspects of the colonial process from the beginning to the end of colonial contact. They use pidgin English in their texts, a language which reflects the way English is actually used by some Nigerians. The 'Three Great African Novelists"— Chinua Achebe (1930), Wole Soyinka (1934) and Amos Tutuola (1920) — describe the impact of European ideas and government on the Africans. Though Achebe and Soyinka wrote to change the society and the world, Tutuola did not exhibit a strong political awareness so as to bring a revolution in African society. But *Palm Wine Drinkard* of Tutuola, opened the floodgates to modern West African writing. His narrative was largely based on Yoruba folk structure woven into the fabric of a different language. Tutuola, Soyinka, Achebe, and Awoonor operate as a writer in traditional aesthetics. In Soyinka's novel *The Interpreters,* each of his major characters—Sagoe, Egbo, Bandele, Se Koni, and Kala — is an interpreter, an artist seeking to infuse a moral balance into a fast disintegrating world. In Achebe's first novel, *Things Fall Apart,* the centre held, for it was only Okonkwo who decided to kill himself. Umuofia refused to commit suicide. In *Arrow of God,* Ezeulu mistook his vengeful will for the will of his god and is struck mad. His refusal to eat Yam spelt hardship on his community, but his people neglected disaster and brought home harvest in the name of his son. The victory was not of Christianity but of Umuaro.

Buchi Emecheta in *The Slave Girl,* Chinua Achebe in *Anthills of the Savannah,* and ken Saro Wiwa in *Home Sweet Home,* have used the narrative technique and imagery to show the changing role of women in Nigerian society. In *The Slave Girl,* one of Emecheta's main themes involving slavery, the assertion is that in Nigerian Society, all women are enslaved to and by men. She presents the Nigerian woman as continuously enslaved to male master figures. Whereas Achebe and Saro-Wiwa present independence for the Nigerian woman as a conceivable possibility.

Both Emecheta and Achebe are Igbo writers, whose characters Okonkwo and Nnu Ego, symbolize, the positive and negative aspects of their tribal culture. The conflict, that they encounter throughout their adult life, is about their nation's tension between tradition and modernity, and through their own struggle to survive, they anticipate Nigeria's struggle for political independence. Money appears in many guises in Chinua's *Anthills of the Savannah* and Awuor Ayoda's *Workday,* which decide the nature of one's work, education, lifestyle, social status, and physical well-being. In the former, money's presence for the central characters is assured and assumed, whereas in the latter, the servant girl Mary toils for 300 shillings a month, all of which she sends home to feed her numerous younger siblings—a tremendous disparity in lifestyles. Some contemporary postcolonial African writers like Flora Nwapa, Buchi Emecheta, Chenjari Hove, Cyprian Ekwensi, and Ngũgĩ wa Thiong'o have described the feminine characters in multiple meanings.

The Democracy's Warrior—Chinua Achebe, is in a quest for transition of African society, from the state of 'anarchy' to the state of 'order' which always had a rich and varied cultural heritage. Achebe's novels develop the theme of "traditional verses change". The *Gyres of Anarchy* focuses on the validity of traditional life and values, and the disruptiveness of change. But even while deploring the imperialists, Achebe seems to suggest that the change is inevitable, and wise men do reconcile themselves to an accommodating change. And so it is possible to show respect to English and Igbo together. He asserts that the diehards who resist and rebel are destined to be destroyed in the process. Trevor Royle in his book *Winds of Change,* writes about the End of Empire in Africa that:

> What is required, perhaps, is a realization that the rule of empire in Africa was not all bad; that government, trade and commerce were helped immeasurably by the participation of the white man and that in many African countries he still has a role to play. Only when that happens can the process of decolonization be put into proper perspective (10).

Achebe is critical about the state of Africa but feels that only the Africans can describe their own country in the best way and give a detailed information about its culture and people. He vehemently admits that Africa which is the origin of various species of mankind, can give much to other nations. He simply expects others to hear the African writers patiently to get a real picture of Africa. Achebe does believe in the proverb that, "Until the lions produce their own historian, the story of the hunt will glorify only the hunter" (Achebe, *Home and Exile* 73). He feels that the writers will have to do something, so that the story of the hunt will also reflect the agony, the travail—the bravery of the lions.

Works Cited

Achebe, Chinua. *Home and Exile*. New York : Anchor, 2000.

______________ *Hopes and Impediments: Selected Essays*. New York: Anchor, 1988.

_____________ *The Trouble with Nigeria.* London: Heinemann, 1983.

Chinua Achebe's Things Fall Apart: A CaseBook. Ed. Isidore Okewho. New York: Oxford University, 2003.

Clarke, John Henrik. "Why Africana History ?" *Race and History.* January 1987 http: // www.raceandhistory.com/historicalviews/2004/ clarke22.html.

"Embodiment in Arican Literature," *English Essays.* 2004 http: // www.englishessays.org.uk/english_essays/ embodiment_african_literature.php.

February, V.A. *Mind Your colour: The 'coloured' stereotype in South African Literature.* London: Kegan Paul, 1981.

Isichei, Elizabeth. *A History of Christianity in Africa: From Antiquity to the present.* London: Cromwell, 1995.

Kawu-Bala, Attahiru. *"Black History." Destroying the Horrors of 500 years: A Review of 500 years later,* 30 March 2007 http: // www.itzcaribbean.com/500 years later.php.

Majumdar, Bimalendu. *JoyceCary: An Existentialist Approach.* New Delhi: 1990.

Mehta, Gurleena and Narang Harish. *Apartheid in Fiction.* New Delhi: Commonwealth, 1990.

Royle, Trevor. *Winds of Change: The End of Empire in Africa.* London: John Murray, 1996.

Soyinka, Wole. *The Burden of Memory, the Muse of Forgiveness.* New York: Oxford University Press, 1999.

Thiong'o, Ngũgĩ wa. *Decolonising the Mind: The Politics of Language in african Literature.* Delhi: Worldview, 1986.

Writing Across Worlds: Contemporary writers talk. Ed. Susheila Nasta. London: Routledge, 2004.

3 Cultural Heritage

The crowning glory of Achebe's novels, is undoubtedly, his aphorisms of oral culture. Chinua Achebe clearly presents the perception of culture in Igbo society and profound cultural dislocation due to arrival of Europeans in Nigeria. He is quite honest in showing the difficult life of the Igbos and makes no attempt to gloss over their problems. But the fact cannot be denied that the Europeans raided and raped the African culture, and then called the Africans as 'primitive'. They became successful in developing inferiority complex in the Africans who now wanted to imbibe the new culture to prove themselves as equals. Professor D. Westermann, in *The African Today* says that the Negros' inferiority complex is particularly intensified among the most educated who must struggle with it unceasingly:

> The wearing of European clothes, whether rags or the most up-to-date style; using European furniture and European forms of social intercourse; adorning the Native language with European expressions; using bombastic phrases in speaking or writing a European language; all these contribute to a feeling of equality with the European and his achievements (qtd.in Fanon, *Black Skin White Masks* 25).

Emmanuel Oblechina, demonstrating the uniqueness and power of embodiment in Achebe's literary work claims that, "Achebe is most successful in expressing his African experience in English and still preserving its African authenticity" ("Embodiment in African Literature"). In his autobiographical essay, "Named for Victoria," Achebe admits that probably he has spoken more words in Igbo than English but has definitely written more words in English than Igbo. Achebe's love for Igbo language can be seen in his novels, where he uses a variety of Igbo words—*Ilo, Agbala, Ogbanje, Osu, Ndichie, Agadin wayi, Efulefu, Egwugwu, Nno, Obi,*

Chukwo, Chi and many more. This he emphasized to show that inspite of the impact of the European culture on the African people, including the writers, their love for their own culture always remained intact.

Achebe asserts that his family lived at the crossroads of culture. On one hand, he was allured by the Church services, and on the other, he was fascinated by the life and rituals of the Igbo people: "Those idols and that food had a strange pull on me in spite of my being such a thorough little Christian..."(Achebe, *Hopes and Impediments* 35). Achebe presents a real picture of the chaos experienced by those born at the crossroads of culture. He shows the conflict of ideology, ethos, behaviour, values, and attitude in between the native society and the white man. Achebe who lived at the crossroads of cultures admits in his novel *Hopes and Impediments*:

> ...The crossroads does have a certain dangerous potency; dangerous because a man might perish there wrestling with multiple-headed spirits, but also he might be lucky and return to his people with the boon of prophetic vision (34).

Folklore, which is an important feature of the Ibo culture, finds ample and appropriate place in the novels of Achebe. He feels that cultures use folklore to pass on great cultural richness, and so it can provide solution to people's questions and problems. He explains to the readers that by the time he comes to the Ibo society in Nigeria, in *No Longer at Ease,* most traditional values disappear. But some of the proverbs show that the moral and spiritual wisdom still remain with the people, such as: "...He who has people is richer than he who has money" (Achebe 91).

Achebe's love for his own culture is quite prominent in his novels, as he depicts beautifully the customs and rituals of the Igbos. He shows that the beauty of the Igbo culture lay on the unity and togetherness on various occasions. He opens before the readers, a beautiful world of Ibo nation, with their perception of culture. His world-famous novel, *Things Fall Apart,* opens with a description about the village of Umuofia, where the Igbos lead a life of gay and happiness. From Umuofia to Mbaino, wrestling was enjoyed, and Okonkwo brought honour to his village, Umuofia. They had time to relax and share their victories. The

Igbos beat the drums on various occasions, and enjoyed music and feasting. Farming being their profession, the Igbos celebrated a lot after the harvest.

Fig 3. Statue of Igbo people

Source: Electronic.

The Igbos showed keen interest in learning the tunes of various instruments like flute, ekwe, udu, and ogene. Achebe shows the urge of the Igbos to develop and progress. In *Things Fall Apart,* during the planting season, Okonkwo worked daily on his farms from cock-crow until the chickens went to roost. His prosperity was visible in his household. Apart from his own hut or *obi,* he had three more huts built for his three wives. Near the barn, he had a 'medicine house' or Shrine where Okonkwo kept the wooden symbols of his personal god—*Chi,* and of his ancestral spirits. He worshipped them with sacrifices of Kola nut, food, and palm wine, and offered prayers to them on behalf of himself, his three wives, and eight children. In Igbo society, sacrifices were given before planting of the crops. In *Things Fall Apart* (TFA), Okonkwo narrates to the priestess, Chika that:

> ...Before I put any crop in the earth, I sacrifice a cock to Ani, the owner of all land. It is the law of our fathers. I also kill a cock at the shrine of Ifejioku, the god of yams (Achebe 16).

In TFA, the centrality of the 'Yam' highlights the tribe's respect for the physical vigour. Among the Ibo people, a person was not known by his father's identity but by his own. In Umuofia, "Age was respected among his people, but achievement was revered"(8). As Okonkwo was brave and courageous, it was said that he ate with the kings and elders.

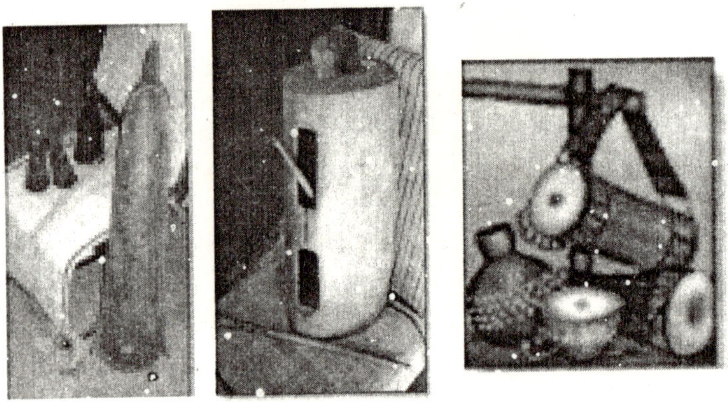

Ogene: Metal Gong *Ekwe: Wooden Drum* *African instruments*

Fig 4. African instruments

Source: Electronic.

Achebe reflects the innocent hearts of the Africans which was full of warmth for the visitors. The Igbos had their own traditional and unique way of welcoming their guests. A Kola which was served to the visitors was broken with a wish or a prayer. And then a lump of chalk was given to them with which each of them drew his personal emblem of upright and horizontal lines on the floor. Some painted their big toe and other marked their face. Okonkwo breaks the kola nut in front of his guests, saying:

> We shall all live. We pray for life, children, a good harvest and happiness. You will have what is good for you and I will have what is good for me. Let the kite perch and let the egret perch too. If one says no the other, let his wing break (Achebe, TFA 17-18).

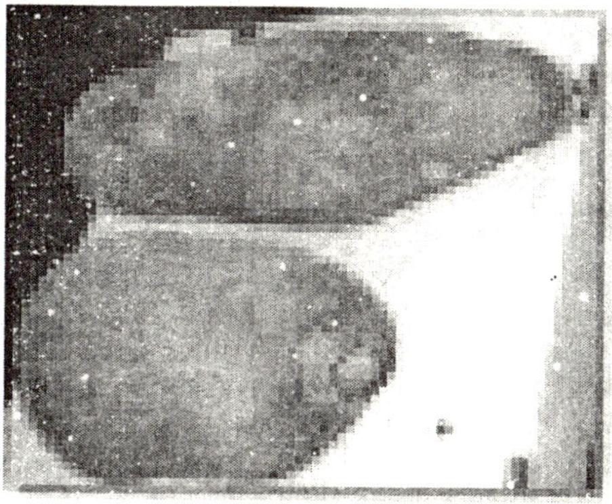

Fig 5. ***Yams,*** **chief food of Igbos**

Source: Electronic

Achebe has well-presented the festivals and the celebrations of the Ibos. A good description of the feast of the New Yam Festival finds place in his novels. It was an occasion for giving thanks to Ani, the earth goddess and the source of all fertility. As per the ritual, on the last night before the festival, yams of the old year were all disposed off by those who still had them, and a good sized seed-yam was offered to the shrine. The New Year began with the tasty fresh yams, and not the shrivelled and fibrous crop of the previous year. In *Things Fall Apart*, "Men and women, young and old, looked forward to the New Yam Festival because it began the season of plenty—the new year" (Achebe 33). The second day of the new year was celebrated by having great wrestling contests in between the villages. In Igbo, this sport was known to have started thirty years ago and was still the liking of all the Igbos. All the contests like wrestling, and great ceremonies and dances like New Yam Festival, Pumpkin Festival, Ozo Dance, Dance by the Ancestral Spirits took place on the *'ilo'*—playground, which was as old as the village itself. Achebe has given a brief description of the Festival of Pumpkin Leaves, in which all the people gathered to celebrate the occasion together. Men brought palm wine in pots and every woman held a bunch of pumpkin leaves in her right hand. In Achebe's novel, *Things Fall Apart,* the citizens of Umuofia revealed their wealth through acts of generosity. During the festival, "every man whose arm was strong..., was expected to invite large numbers of guests from far and wide" (34). The love of the Igbos for their relations is quite clear by the way they invited their friends and their relations from the neighbouring villages, and by the huge quantity of food that they prepared on special occasions. In *Arrow of God,* the Igbos believed that "...he is a fool who treats his brother worse than a stranger" (Achebe 95).

The Igbo's concern for freshness and hygiene can be seen in the preparation of food. In *Things Fall Apart,* Achebe has shown that before cooking food, all the cooking-pots, calabashes, and wooden bowls were thoroughly washed, especially the wooden mortar in which the yam was pounded. Yam *foo-foo,* vegetable soup, bitter-leaf soup, *egusi* soup, and wine tapped from raffia palm were the chief food in the celebration. In *No longer at Ease,* Achebe depicts Obi's love for Nigerian food, in spite of the fact that he had spent five years in England. At a restaurant, when Joseph asked Obi if he wanted Nigerian food, Obi said:

> Of course. I have been dying to eat pounded yams and bitter-leaf soup. In England we made to do with semolina, but it isn't the same thing... I am sick of boiled potatoes (Achebe 39).

Igbos craving for beauty and fashion can be seen in Achebe's novels. In *Things Fall Apart,* the women scrubbed the walls and huts with red earth until they reflected light. In *No longer at Ease,* gay temporary sheds were erected in front of derelict houses and lit with brilliant fluorescent tubes for the celebration of an engagement or marriage, or birth or the death of an old relative. Then patterns were drawn on them in white, yellow and dark green. The Igbo women painted themselves with cam wood and used a black dye [*uli*] to draw beautiful black patterns on their stomachs and on their backs. The children were also decorated, especially their hair, which was shaved in beautiful patterns. Men wore toga over loincloth and on head an ozo cap girdled with a leather band from which an eagle feather pointed slightly backwards. They also held along, iron walking staff with a sharp, spear-like lower end.

Fig. 6. Mask with uli

Source: Electronic.

Achebe describes the Igbo culture very beautifully and aptly through his characters. In TFA, he gives a description about Okonkwo's love for the Igbo traditions and customs even in adversities. When he was exiled for seven years for killing a clansman, he found shelter in his mother's village, Mbanta. Though Okonkwo was distorted and frustrated as he had to sacrifice the name and the glory which he earned all these years, he did not forget his culture to thank his mother's kinsmen before he left Mbanta. All the *umunna* were invited to the feast—all the descendants of Okolo, who had lived about two hundred years before. There was *foo-foo* and yam pottage, *egusi* soup and bitter-leaf soup, and pots and pots of palm-wine and meat. In the Igbo culture, Akwu Nro was a little ritual performed by the widows as a memorial offering to their departed husbands. Achebe, in his novel *Arrow of God,* mentions about widows in Umuachala who prepared *foo-foo* and palm nut soup on the night of Akwu Nro and put outside their huts. Seeing the bowls empty in the morning, it was believed that the husbands came from Ani-Mmo and ate the food.

In Igbo society, each ethnic group [most popular ones—Yoruba, Ibo, and Hausa-Fulani] had a Shrine dedicated to the deities. The Oracle of the Hills and the Caves find a prominent place in *Things Fall Apart,* showing the religious beliefs of the Igbo ancestry. The Igbos obeyed the directions and instructions given by Agbala, the priestess. Some people said that they had heard the spirits flying and flapping their wings against the roof of the cave. Whatever their beliefs may be, the Igbos have been depicted as simple and innocent beings. In TFA, Achebe has shown the towns like Umuofia, Mbaino, Mbanta, Abame, etc., as autonomous communities where people lived peacefully with one another. In case of a dispute, the councils of elders resolved the matter. Achebe's empathy with his ancestral culture is even more evident in the harmonies that he reveals between the people and their environment:

> The drums were still beating, persistent and unchanging. Their sound was no longer a separate thing from the living village. It was like the pulsation of its heart. It throbbed in the air, in the sunshine, and even in the trees, and filled the village with excitement (TFA 40).

Achebe also depicts some cultural problems like favouritism, laziness, tardiness, and disunity among the villages of the Ibo nation. In *Things Fall Apart,* Okonkwo's father, Unoke is an epitome of failure and laziness as he could not think of the future. He was called Agbala—one who had taken no title, or a woman, whereas Okonkwo was diligent and so could achieve many things in life.

Achebe throws some light on the beliefs of the Igbos which, no doubt, shows that they were superstitious and orthodox. Though the Igbos have been shown by Achebe as very brave and courageous, they had a fear of darkness and wild animals. It seems to be quite strange that men like Okonkwo, who did not fear at the time of killing Ikemefuna, men who did not fear killing of twins, had fear of darkness. Achebe presents Okonkwo as a great man, whose powers were universally acknowledged. But he also mentions that though he had love for hunting, his guns never shot even a rat.

But with the course of time, the Igbo culture lost its uniqueness. In 1868, bonny traditional religion declined, the previously sacred iguanas were killed, and by the 1880s, the temple of skulls dedicated to the war god, Ikuba, was falling into ruins. Achebe over-emphasizes the fact that inspite of the problems which Igbo society experienced, before coming of the Europeans, it stood as a nation. But with the arrival of the white man, 'Gyres of Anarchy' displaced the native societies, and changed the Igbo's perception of culture. In *Gathering Seaweed,* Kwame Nkrumah of Ghana, critically expresses his thoughts about the culture brought by the Europeans:

> The impact of western culture on the African mind brought in its train as much bad as good. Offences like forgery, bribery and corruption, for instance, were practically unknown in our early society (56).

But whatever the Igbos beliefs and practices were, they have been shown to have loved them. Achebe makes no attempt to express his own feelings and thoughts about them, but reveals the truth about the Igbo society. Achebe also depicts the negative aspects of the African culture. In *Things Fall Apart,* he shows the infamous

Clitoridectomy of twins whom Igbo tradition regards as an abomination [in which the twins were left to die in the bush]. It also shows the ritual killing of the boy hostage, Ikemefuna by Okonkwo, who sheltered him for almost three years and treated him as his own son. When Okonkwo's wife, Ekwefi's second child died, the medicine-man told him that the child was an *ogbanje*—one of those wicked children who when died, entered their mother's wombs to be born again. Achebe's novels also show disunity among the clans who fought over trivial matters. In TFA, Okonkwo and his friend Obierika discuss about their neighbouring villages, Abame and Aninta. They talk about the titled men who climbed trees and pounded foo-foo for their wives. They also criticize another clan saying:

> All their customs are upside-down. They do not decide bride-price as we do, with sticks. They haggle and bargain as if they were buying a goat or a cow in the market (Achebe 67).

A terrifying spectacle can be seen in Achebe's novel *Things Fall Apart,* when nine of the greatest masked ancestral spirits in the clan come out together, each representing a village in the clan. They had smoked raffia body, huge wooden face painted white, with round hollow eyes and charred teeth that were as big as a man's fingers. Their leader had two powerful horns on his head who was called 'Evil Forest'.

Fig 7. Ancestral mask

Source: Electronic.

Achebe talks of the Nwaka of Umunneora who had a great Mask which he assumed on Idemili festival and other important occasions:

> The Mask was called Ogalanya or Man of Riches, and...crowds of people from all the villages and their neighbours came to the ilo of Umunneora to see this great Mask bedecked with mirrors and rich cloths of many colours (Achebe, *Arrow of God* 40).

In *Arrow of God,* Achebe talks of Edogo, Ezeulu's first son, who used to carve masks in his hut which produced a certain ambience and gave power to his fingers. Most of the masks were of fierce, aggressive ancestral spirits with horns and teeth of the size of the fingers.

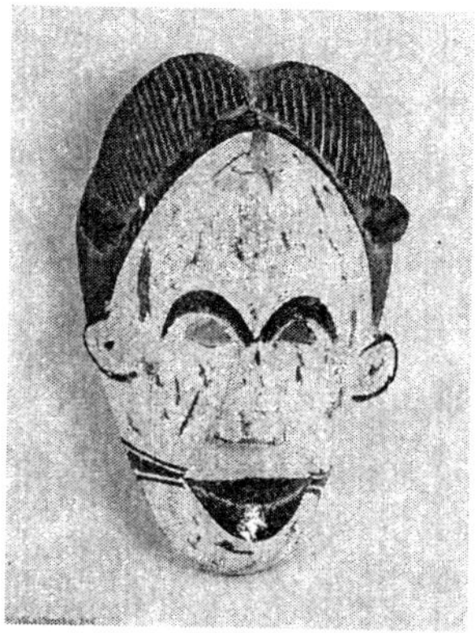

Fig 8. Beautiful Maiden

Source: Electronic.

Only few masks belonged to maiden–spirits—delicately beautiful. It was the belief in Umuaro that all the Udala trees were sacred to the ancestral spirits, and if anyone picked from the tree, would have to wipe off their footsteps with heavy fines and sacrifice. This belief of the Igbos reminds one of the Indians' belief in the sanctity of trees. Indians do worship trees like peepal and banyan, as they believe in the myths related to it.

The white man brought about a change in the cultural perception of the Igbo people. The Europeans brought with them western culture and education, and also a new religion for the Igbos. They needed time to change the age-long practices of the people. But they did not make it evident for the Igbos to know about their intentions. In his novels, Achebe has shown few of the elders who could anticipate the reason for the white man's arrival. In *Things Fall Apart,* Obierika, Okonkwo's friend could prophecy the demise of the village of Umuofia. In answer to Okonkwo's question "Does the white man understand our custom about land?" Obierika responded:

> How can he when he does not even speak our tongue? But he says that our customs are bad; and our own brothers who have taken up his religion also say that our customs are bad...now he has won our brothers, and our clan can no longer act like one. He has put a knife on the things that held us together and we have fallen apart (160).

Fig 9. Change in cultural perception

Source: Electronic.

Achebe presents the degeneration of native values and unending chaos in Africa. The Christian missionaries disrupted the cultural life of the Igbos. They recruited church members from along the margines of Ibo society—like the *osus* who were the outcasts. Once converted, people grappled in various ways with the relationship between their new faith and cultural inheritance; and the needs and obligations of their immediate environment. Despite this, the Africans could not remain uninfluenced by their own culture:

> ...African Christians inevitably understood Christianity in terms of their own culture, and incorporated many of its insights...scholarly opinion is sharply divided as to when this becomes inculturation, and when syncretism (Isichei, *A History of Christianity* 46).

In her book *A History of Christianity,* Elizabeth Isichei also talks about some missionaries who adopted the African lifestyles. But they did overlook cultural richess of Africa and were convinced of their own superiority. They acquired fluency in Igbo language to preach their religion. They had taken the inferiority of the natives for granted. In *Things Fall Apart,* when Okonkwo returns just after seven years of exile, the village seems to be unrecognizable for Okonkwo. The 'Things' had changed. The indigenous tradition and heritage got swept, resulting in cultural dislocation and loss of identity. The Igbos had been attracted towards the new culture, new religion, and the new government:

> The new religion and government and the trading stores were very much in the people's eyes and minds...even they talked and thought about little else, and certainly not about Okonkwo's return (Achebe 165).

Achebe talks of his parents in *Home and Exile,* who had Christian beliefs, but still loved the Igbo people and their mannerisms. His father received his peers and relations—Christian or not, with Kola nut and palm-wine, and his mother entertained the visitors amicably. Achebe shows the impact of Western education and culture on the Igbos, especially the youth. In *No Longer at Ease,* Achebe reflects the problem of corruption in 1950s Lagos. The craving for money and other material possessions promoted corruption in the Igbo society. Obi on seeing the corrupt practices, longs to go back to Umuofia and feels ashamed of studying English for his degree. He had love for Ibo language and the people who spoke it. He felt humiliated to speak to his own countrymen in English language, especially in presence of proud owners of that language. Obi felt: "Let them [people] come to Umuofia now and listen to the talk of men who made a great art of conservation" (Achebe, *No Longer at Ease* 57). Obi who believed that the civil service was corrupt because of the so-called experienced men at the top, himself falls prey to the western culture. He experiences the financial crisis as he wanted to live up to an inflated image, wanted to show off his position in the civil service. Obi became a member of an exclusive club whose members greeted one another with:

> How's the car behaving ?" did they expect him to turn round and answer: "I'm sorry, but my car is off the road. You see I couldn't pay my insurance premium"?...that was quite unthinkable (Achebe, *No Longer at Ease* 113).

In the novel, Achebe further says that though the society of Umuofia was against Obi, it could be realized that it was not totally against corruption. It only wanted a man to learn how and when to receive the bribe. The president of Umuofia Progressive Union criticizes Obi for his inability to judge the opportune time for receiving bribe, and talks about corruption openly:

> ...it was a thing of shame for a man in the senior service to go to prison for twenty pounds..."I am against people reaping where they have not sown. But we have a saying that if you want to eat a toad you should look for a fat and juicy one" (*No Longer at Ease* 6-7).

The novels of Achebe reflect the cultural conflict which was used by the white man to their advantage. In *Arrow of God,* Wintabota, meddles in the Ibo nation war of Afo between the Umuaro and the Okperi but gives the decision in favour of Okperi. And thus Igbo's claim of self-reliance and self-determination was challenged. Achebe also reflects Christianity which causes another cultural conflict, a spiritual conflict in the villages via converts: "Go and burn your mothers' genitals," said one of the priests. "The men were seized and beaten until they streamed with blood" (TFA 141).

Achebe has well-presented the consequences of both the acceptance as well as the rejection of the new faith and religion. In *Things Fall Apart,* Enoch's new faith led him to unmask an egwugwu in public, the greatest crime in Umuofia, which made the band of egwugwu convert Enoch's compound into a desolate heap. On the other hand, Okonkwo's lack of respect and reverence for the new religion and culture, led to his catastrophic end—he hanged himself on a tree and was buried like a dog. Isichei cites similar instances in *A History of Christianity,* which shows the impact of the new religion on the converts:

> Some converts risked their lives by attacks on masqueraders, whose costume was an obvious physical manifestation of traditional belief. Others attempted to create a Christian form of Ogboni, the secret Yoruba cult of the sacred Earth. Some renounced traditional titles, while Idigo of Aguleri acquired a superannuated horse, with the help of the Holy Ghost Fathers, and took the rare and prestigious title *ogbu anyinya,* Horse killer (159).

Ezeulu, the main protagonist of Achebe's *Arrow of God,* tries his best to move with the change taking place in Igbo society. He says: "I am like the bird Eneke-nti-oba .... Men of today have learnt to shoot without missing and so I have learnt to fly without perching" (46). Achebe, through his character Ezeulu, wants to remind the readers of the significance of change in one's outlook. In *Arrow of God,* Ezeulu sends his son Oduche, to the missionaries to be his eye there. This is because he could think of tomorrow, he could think of the new perception of culture due to the arrival of white man. No doubt, Ezeulu had respect for his own culture. He did believe in the custom of Umuaro, where a man who killed python, was required to placate the deity, Idemili, by arranging a funeral for snake as elaborate as a man's funeral. So when Ezeulu's son committed sin by putting the snake into the box, he had to cleanse the six villages of the sin by sacrifices.

In "Chike's School Days", in *Girls at War,* Achebe highlights the change which comes in the cultural perception of the Igbos. Chike, who is the son of an Osu woman, whom Chike's father marries in the name of Christianity, was brought up in the ways of the white man. His day began with the prayers and hymn-singing and ended with the same. Achebe depicts the transition which comes in the life of Igbos due to the coming of missionaries. Converts were often attracted by the belief that Christianity was stronger than the evil:

> In the Christian village, there are no witches, and the witches have no power there; the pagans say, that as soon as a witch becomes a Christian, her witchcraft is extinguished (qtd. in Isichei, *A History of Christianity* 168).

Osus who could not raise their shaggy head in the presence of the free born, who were despised and almost spat on, were accepted by the Igbos due to the acceptance by the white man. The cultural crisis in the hearts of the Igbos is prominent who become helpless in the presence of new culture and tradition. In the short story collection *Girls at War*, when Chike's grandmother, who takes the name of Elizabeth, goes to meet a diviner to share his discontentment, he says:

> Your son has joined the white man's religion. And you too in your old age when you should know better. And do you wonder that he is stricken with insanity? Those who gather ant-infested faggots must be prepared for the visit of lizards (Achebe 39).

The degeneration of the moral values can be seen in M.A. Nanga, the protagonist of Achebe's novel *A Man of the People*. Chief Nanga has been shown as a corrupt politician who knew how to give and take bribe. As he was strong, and powerful, he could take Odili's girlfriend to his bed when Odili himself was at home. In his official residence, Chief Nanga had seven bedrooms and seven bathrooms, one for each day of the week. Chief Nanga was a hypocrat who knew how to flatter people. He reminds the young people that if they respect him today as a king, others would respect them when their turn comes.

Europeans knew what the Igbo people wanted, they knew that without the help of Igbos, they could not disintegrate their society. That is the reason, corruption was promoted and encouraged in modern Igbo society. In *Arrow of God*, the court clerks appointed by British took advantage of their fellow Igbos through bribery and money lending. In *A Man of the People*, the issue which Max raises infront of Odili Samalu throws light on the corruption being encouraged by the Europeans in Nigeria:

> ...Odili, that British Amalgamated has paid out four hundred thousand pounds to P.O.P. to fight this election?

> Yes, and we also know that the Americans have been even more generous... (Achebe 127-128).

Achebe has shown bribe-receiving as a part of the changed Igbo culture. In *A Man of the People,* Achebe has presented Mr. Nanga as the best example of a corrupted individual who knew how to crucify innocent men and assassinate their character. As a minister, he knew how to offer bribe to the people for the votes and also to the journalists for writing good about him. Mr. Odo, Edna's father is full of greed and enjoys receiving gifts from Chief Nanga, his son-in-law—a man of fifty, for the reason that he is getting his young daughter married to an old man. Edna's father says:

> Our people say : if you fail to take away a strong man's sword when he is on the ground, will you do it when he gets up...? No, my daughter. Leave me and my in-law. He will bring and bring and I will eat until I am tired. And thanks to the Man Above he does not lack what to bring (Achebe, *A Man of the People* 93).

In his Postcolonial novel *Anthills of the Savannah,* Achebe shows the influence of British tradition on the Kangan elite culture and its life. The country's new leaders were the products of the imposed European culture. Ikem, Chris, Sam, and Beatrice who were all educated in British schools, modelled their lives and beliefs on the European British lifestyle. Both Chris and Ikem return to Kangan after their college education in the U.K., with the hope to build a vibrant democratic nation, but gets suck in the web of corruption and authoritarianism that has been so typical of postcolonial Africa. Of the three schoolboy chums-Chris, Ikem, and Sam, it was Sam who especially admired his European Predecessors:

> He was fascinated by the customs of the English, especially their well-to-do classes and enjoyed playing at their foibles. When he told me about his elegant pipe which he had spent a whole morning choosing in a Mayfair shop I could see that he was not taking himself seriously at all.... Of course one may well question the appropriateness of these attitudes in a Head of State (Achebe, *Anthills of the Savannah* 45).

Achebe is not narrow-minded and bitter and does not object to the discovery of and learning of the new religion and culture. In his novels, he presents clear picture of the new society and develops our understanding of it. Achebe does not try to impose Nigerian culture upon a European audience, but he also expects that the European culture should not be imposed on an unwilling Nigerian clan. In *Things Fall Apart,* Achebe shows that the missionaries simply walked into the midst of the tribe with their interpreters, and "told them that they worshipped false gods, gods of wood and stone" (131). And thousands of years of worshipping unchanged deities, the white man verbally commands them, "Leave your wicked ways and false gods" (132).

Achebe constantly views the colonial relationship as "Master and Slave" relationship. He expresses his contempt for the missionary work and colonial project by making them seem "mad", and gives a reason for much laughing and ridiculing. He also hints at more sinister aspect of their arrival, that is, the doom of the Igbo society which could not be so easily anticipated by the Igbos. Chinua Achebe in his works has shown the ceremonies and the culture which bound the tribe together, and which the missionaries targeted to ignore. What Achebe objects to, is the forceful conversion to Christianity. The ways adopted by the missionaries were crooked, they even bribed and blackmailed the innocent villagers.

In *Things Fall Apart,* Achebe talks of the white missionary which had set up a school to teach young Christians how to read and write. It infers that the unconverted heathen had no right to gain knowledge. So the transition had started from Nigerian precolonial orature, towards a more Eurocentric culture. Achebe does not forget to show the converts' own self-centered ulterior motives for joining the missionaries by accepting the church and the formal education:

> The newly-arrived missionary could not be an instant expert on African languages and cultures, and the incarnation of Christianity in different African cultures involved a great multiplicity of choices that, ultimately, could be made only by Africans themselves (Isichei, *A History of Christianity* 82).

Nwoye in *Things fall Apart* is more attracted by the "rollicking tunes of evangelism" than by the doctrines of Christianity. Nneka also has her own reason for conversion. She goes to the missionaries to save her unborn child, as her two sets of twins were killed by the tribe already. A similar incident is quoted by Isichei:

> Bribrina was expelled from her home in Patani, a village in the Niger Delta, when she gave birth to twins. She was rescued, with her babies, by an Isoko trader who married her, and she pioneered Christianity among his people (*A History of Christianity* 156).

So it was their personal concerns and weaknesses which encouraged the Igbos to accept the new culture. It was not that the African people had heard of culture for the first time from Europeans, or their societies were mindless. They had a philosophy of great depth and value and beauty, that they had poetry and above all they had dignity. In *Things Fall Apart*, Achebe never accepts that the new culture and religion could be fully recognized and accepted even by the converts:

> In the debate between the British missionary (Brown) and a local savant (Akunna), it becomes clear to the former that the foreign culture has little to teach the indigenous African in terms of theological sophistication; the goals of domination will have to be achieved by other methods (Ed. Okpewho, *A Case Book* 26).

Achebe accepts that the Igbo culture was not without flaws. In the life of the Africans, on one hand, there was happiness and prosperity, on the other, there were superstitious beliefs and fear of the unseen. He does not deny the fact that the Western culture and education paved way to their growth and development. But even the Africans could influence the Europeans by exhibiting their strength of unity and togetherness:

> ...it is clear that just as Christianity has been influenced by insights from African cultures, African religions have absorbed intimations from Christianity (Isichei, *A History of Christianity* 7).

Works Cited

Achebe, Chinua. *A Man of the People*. New York: Anchor, 1966.

______________ *Anthills of the Savannah*.New York: Anchor, 1987.

______________ *Arrow of God*. New York: Anchor, 1974.

______________ *Hopes and Impediments:Selected Essays*. New York: Anchor, 1988.

______________ *Girls at War and other Stories*. New York:Anchor, 1973.

______________ *No Longer at Ease*. New York: Anchor, 1960.

______________ *Things Fall Apart*. New Delhi:Allied, 2004.

Chinua Achebe's *Things Fall Apart: A CaseBook*. Ed. Isidore Okpewho. New York: Oxford University, 2003.

"Embodiment in African Literature."*English Essays*. 2004 *http: // www. englishessays. org.uk/ english_ essays /embodiment_african_ literature.php*.

Fanon Frantz, *Black Skin White Masks*. New York: Grove, 1967.

Gathering Seaweed: African Prison Writing. Ed. Jack Mapanje. London: Heinemann, 2002.

Isichei, Elizabeth. *A History of Christianity in Africa : From Antiquity to the Present*. London: Cromwell, 1995.

4 Impact of Colonialism on Literary Transformation

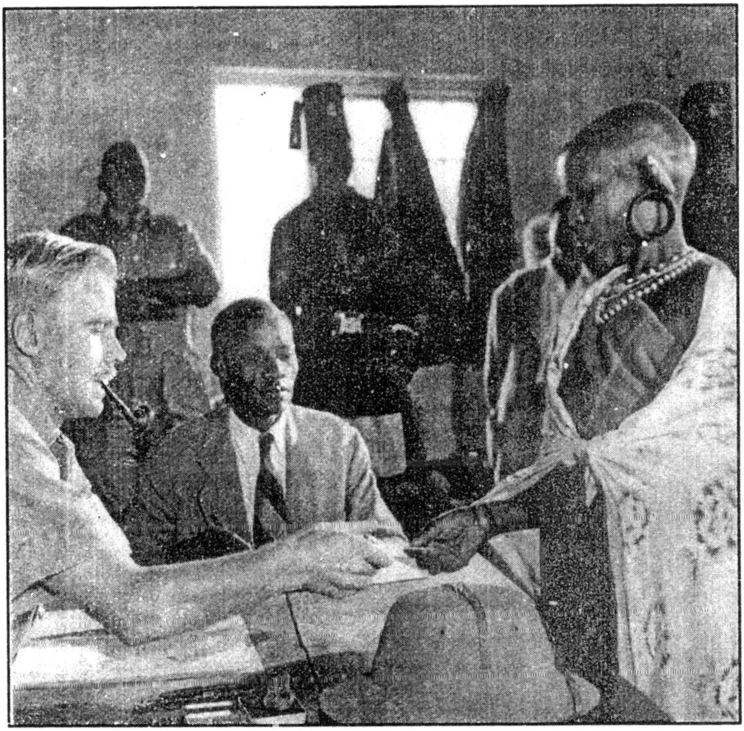

Fig 10. ***Colonial Rule in Africa,*** **from Back jacket illustration, in Trevor Royle,** ***Winds of Change*** **(London: John Murray, 1996)**

Chinua Achebe describes the pain and agony experienced by Africans due to the colonial rule. His novels depict the Igbos as the victims of the European colonialism and industrialism. So silently the Europeans came to the shores of Africa, that the

Africans could not realise their intentions. The Igbo people were astonished and surprised by the ways of the white man, but were not very prompt in their actions. In *Things Fall Apart,* Achebe presents the Igbos merely as the spectators of the new faith, and the new religion. The novel shows the helplessness of the indigenous people in the hands of the missionaries and the white man. Igbos have been shown as having no option than to accept the new culture.The colonial impact could also be seen in Chinua's novel, *Arrow of God* where the Igbos have been shown as accepting the new religion out of their own free-will. The natives could anticipate the growth and progress of their village by adoption of Western education and culture. Ezeulu sends his son Oduche to be his 'ears' at the Christian mission, saying :

> If there is nothing in it, you will come back. But if there is something there you will bring home my share. The world is like a Mask dancing. If you want to see it well you do not stand in one place (Achebe, *Arrow of God* 46).

In *No Longer at Ease,* Achebe takes us a step further to show the impact of colonialism on the Africans. The protagonist has been shown as the product of colonial rule. Obi Okonkwo was sponsored by the whole village to attain English education at England. This shows that by this time, the Igbos had fully understood that the Europeans could pull them out of the state of backwardness. In *Anthills of the Savannah,* the protagonists are shown as active members of the new government after attaining the western education. Thus Achebe slowly takes us through various stages of colonialism which aimed at enslaving Africa's freedom. Achebe presents Igbos as primitive and unsophisticated natives who merely mocked the arrival of the strangers. V.A. February, in *Mind Your Colour* quotes similar instances about early inhabitants—Hottentots and Bushmen when they were encountered by the Portuguese, and later on by the Dutch. There are indications in history that the original inhabitants on seeing the Europeans on their land, danced and sang, and were prepared to exchange gifts. On seeing the strangers they came with twelve cattle, oxen, and cows, and some four or five sheep. They even played flutes in a very harmonized way so as to welcome them. No doubt, February in his book, mentions that the inhabitants were not happy own seeing the strangers, but says that there is little evidence of how they actually felt. Likewise, Achebe in his novels, does not give much indication about the reactions of the natives. Achebe takes us back to the seventeeth century, where the inhabitants were naive and unwise, to anticipate the motives of the white. So what is true of James Matthews's description of the first encounter between black and white to unmask the white deception, is also true of their first encounter in *Things Fall Apart:*

> We watched the white man's arrival
> in strange-shaped ships we did not know.
> now we have become trespassers
> on the shores of our land
>
> (qtd.in February, *Mind your Colour* 34).

Nothing could be more torturous for a person than to become a stranger in one's own land. Best example could be of Mohammad Ali –Cassius Clay, the Olympic gold winner in heavy weight championship. Like any other African, his dream was to get respect from the whites. He struggled for six years to find that the Olympic Gold was of no worth for the blacks, as it could not win them respect in their own land. So he took a firm decision to throw the medal into the Ohio River. The plight of the Africans can be well-understood by the Indians who also had become the strangers in their own land during the British rule.

Achebe had not yet appeared on the literary scene when *Mister Johnson* was written by Joyce Cary. Joyce's novel which centered on the Colonial Africa of 1913-20, was written during the hey-day of British colonialism. Both Achebe and Cary show the arrogant superiority of the white, and the servility of the black. But the former differs much from the latter. Achebe's characters fight against colonial rule, whereas Cary shows Mister Johnson, a black being shot by the white man cum god father Rudbeck, out of his own free-will. It seems that an English writer has made fun of the blacks by showing the Africans as noble savages and buffoons.

Achebe makes the readers feel the change or the transition which takes place in African society, the change which eroded almost every aspect of their traditional life. He talks of the necessity for 'Cultural Exchange' in order to develop partnership between Europe and Africa. He accepts the fact that the partnership in between the black and the white has always been of a horse and a rider. In his book, *Hopes and Impediments*, Achebe asserts that for centuries, Europe has considered the Africans as a beast of burden which automatically rules out the possibility of a dialogue. He feels that Europe and America became rich due to slave trade and colonialism:

> The relationship between Europe and Africa is very old and also very special. The coasts of North Africa and Southern Europe interacted intimately to produce the beginnings of modern European civilization. Later, and much less happily, Europe engaged Africa in the tragic misalliance of the slave trade and colonialism to lay the foundations of modern European and American industrialism and wealth (Achebe 22).

Achebe opposes others' viewpoint that the Igbos are backward and undeveloped tribe. He does not want to call Igbo people as a 'tribe' but as a 'nation', as he feels that they are not primitive and share many cultural traits. In his book *Home and Exile*, Achebe proudly asserts that they speak one language which has scores of major and minor dialects. He also feels that as they do not have one recognized leader, their social and political identity is established. He presents the Igbos as simple and innocent people who formed a nation before coming of the white man. Achebe says that in precolonial times, Igbo nation had hundreds of independent towns and villages. The menfolk carried out their affairs according to the title or rank, which they attained in society, and also on the basis of their age or occupation. He adds that the womenfolk was basically involved in domestic responsibilities as well as the management of the scores of four-day and eight-day markets. These markets gathered crowd from the entire region and even from its neighbourhood.

In *Home and Exile*, Achebe writes that his father was the first Christian convert in his village. He asserts that his parents were sometimes uncompromising in their Christian belief. But he even admits that it was his Christian parents who made him realize the significance of Africa's culture, "...I learned much of what I know and have come to value about my history and culture"(11). Chinua Achebe's love and faith in the African culture is quite prominent in his novels. He makes us understand that the people of Nigeria had their own beliefs and customs which the white man broke apart:

> Today greatness has changed its tune. Titles are no longer great, neither are barns or large numbers of wives and children. Greatness is now in the things of the white man. And so we too have changed our tune. We are the first in all the nine villages to send our son to the white man's land (Achebe, *No Longer at Ease* 62).

Achebe states that Igbos had superstitious beliefs, but these beliefs were their own, there was no guiding force from behind. Igbos could derive happiness and pleasure from small things. Even the showers and breeze could give them happiness, and the children ran about singing, "The rain is falling, the sun is shining,/Alone Nnadi is cooking and eating" (Achebe, *Things Fall Apart* 32). Achebe shows a strong bond of friendship among the Igbos. The way they showed warmth to the visitors and the way they gathered on different occasions show their love for each other. The sharing of food on New Yam Festival, Pumpkin Festival, and all other important occasions shows their concern for each other. Wrestling gave them a chance to compete with others and earn recognition. They sang in praise and clapped their hands in support of their contestants:

> Who will wrestle for our village?
> Okafo will wrestle for our village.
> Has he thrown a hundred men?
> He has thrown four hundred men.
> Has he thrown a hundred Cats?
> He has thrown four hundred Cats.
> Then send him word to fight for us
> (Achebe, *Things Fall Apart* 46).

Achebe provides its readers an opportunity to understand African culture and religion. He takes us through various ceremonies which make us realize the beauty of the Igbo culture. Benedict Chiaka Njoku claims that, "in the world of reality from which Achebe abstracts, the Ibo culture stresses the worth of every man and every woman" ("Embodiment in African Literature"). Achebe also shows the anarchy or the lawlessness in African society with the coming of the Europeans. He depicts the pain experienced by the Igbos due to the strategies and tactics of Europeans to conquer and colonize the land, knowledge, and minds of the indigenous people. The Missionaries who came to Africa in the nineteenth century had little success in the beginning due to the high mortality rates and mistaken mission strategy. But they finally became successful in their domination of Africa. As they could not be an instant expert on African language and cultures, they had to face many problems in fulfilment of their motives:

> In vain with lavish kindness
> The gifts of God are shown,
> The heathen in his blindness
> Bows down to wood and stone
>
> (Isichei, *A History of Christianity* 82).

Achebe in his novels, reflects the missionaries who were penetrated with the thought that the 'Dark Continent' was a cursed land. For them black was 'evil' and white was 'sacred'. They were determined to influence the African minds by imposition of the new beliefs and traditions. In *Things Fall Apart* (TFA), Achebe shows the arrival of the missionaries which causes considerable stir in the village of Mbanta. It seems quite amazing that though the Igbos had heard stories about the strange men who were transporting the Igbo slaves to European nations, the strange men gather around the missionaries to listen to their dialect. They were ignorant of the fact that Europe was busy laying the foundations of European and American industrialism:

> We have heard stories about white men who made the powerful guns and the strong drinks and took slaves away across the seas, but no one thought the stories were true (Achebe, TFA 127).

Achebe presents Igbos as simple beings. Though the missionaries criticized their god—'Chukwu' and claimed superiority of their own 'God', the Igbos did not lose their temper. They simply laughed and called the missionaries 'mad'. Achebe, no doubt, mentions that the missionaries persevered, and so could be received by the rulers [men of high title and the elders] of Mbanta. Achebe rather seems to show that both the Igbos and the missionaries persevered, had much patience, and so one could dictate the other. In Kenya, among the Luo of Central Nyanza, the forecasters had said of the white people:

> If you touch them the skin will remain in your hand because they are very soft. But they will come with thunderstorms and they will burn the people (Ed. Mapanje, *Gathering Seaweed* 8).

Achebe shows contentment and satisfaction in the Igbos who were an integral part of the African society. They had no grudge or complaint against the white man. The Igbos were merely surprised by their courage, as the white man could prove their god to be wrong. They were rather attracted by the new religion and government, and the trading stores. They wanted to grow and to prosper. They could not anticipate that the strangers who had come from far-off land, could change their religion, change their culture, and could change their lives. The Ibos were not intelligent enough to understand the motives of the white man who possessed a lot of tolerance to impose their will on the people of Nigeria. The Igbos on certain occasions could not restrain their emotions and "And so they [some fearless people] killed the white man and tied his iron horse to their sacred tree because it looked as if it would run away to call the man's friends" (TFA 125). Achebe shows that the wisdom of the Igbo society lay basically on the elders. He exhibits the respect which the elders got as they talked wisely on different occasions. They used the proverbs at appropriate time and place. When the clan of Abame is wiped out by the white man on the Afo day, a big market day, Uchendu in Mbanta rightly remarks that, "Never kill a man who says nothing. Those men of Abame were fools. What did they know about the man?" (TFA 126).

Chinua has pictured the missionaries who built their church in various villages and were quite contented to win a handful of converts in the beginning whom the villagers called 'efulefu'—worthless, empty men—without title. In *Things Fall Apart*, six missionaries and a white man tried their best to convince the people by saying that they were also their brothers, as they were all sons of God. They told them about this new God, the creator of all the world, and the men and women. The clans were greatly influenced by the speech of the white man who claimed that they had been sent by the 'Great God' to change their wicked ways. And also to turn to them so that they may be saved when they die. Achebe talks of Christianity, the new religion which could capture the hearts and the minds of the Igbos. They accepted the New God as 'real' and 'supreme'. A rowing song which was recorded among the Tonga of Lake Malawi and the Shire River, was also true of Igbos:

> I have no Mother.
> I have no Father,
> Who will take care of me but our Mother, Maria?
> (qtd.in Isichei, *A History of Christianity* 70).

The missionaries who were perceived as magicians and diviners could attract the children to schools. For them Africans were all ignorant children. They subsidized school education for boys and opened many schools in various remote villages. The literates became Christians just because everyone was becoming a Christian:

> What drew two-thirds of the population of Angola, and over half the population of Zaire to Christianity, despite mission ethnocentricity and racism? The most obvious factor was the missions' near monopoly of education. The fascination with literacy in the late nineteenth century led people to treasure fragments of printed paper, or embark on 'crooked calligraphy' (qtd.in Isichei, *A History of Christianity* 198).

Achebe does not impose on the readers that the new religion and the new culture was bad and evil, but leaves it on them to understand and judge the change taking place in the Igbo society. The fact cannot be denied that more than the words of the missionaries, the Ibo people got influenced by the gay and rollicking tunes of evangelism, which had the power of plucking at the silent hearts. The missionaries could rule over the Igbo people by proving their superstitious beliefs wrong. In *Things Fall Apart*, they could construct their church on the plot of evil land which was the burial ground, and could show their victory by winning the converts. With increased trade, the colonial enterprise could also consolidate its authority and power to protect its interests:

> The white man had indeed brought a lunatic religion, but he had also built a trading store and for the first time palm-oil and kernel became things of great price, and much money flowed into Umuofia (Achebe 161).

Chinua depicts personal concerns in his novels, for showing the change in the attitude of the Igbo people, and getting allured by the missionaries. In *Things Fall Apart*, Nneka, the wife of a prosperous farmer, was the first woman convert, as each time she had borne twins, they were immediately thrown away into the bad bush as per the custom. In some ways, it can be said that the Christian God stood firmly on the side of human behaviour who said that the twins were not evil, and must no longer be abandoned in the forest to die. It was but natural for such an unhappy woman whose heart broke into shreds at every birth, to find refuge in the church which showed her a new hope. Even Nwoye, the first son of Okonkwo was haunted by few questions in his young soul: the question of the twins crying in the bush, and the Ikemefuna who was killed by his father after sheltering him for three years. And it was the poetry of the new religion which captivated Nwoye, and he fled to join the Christians to which Mr. Kiaga, the incharge of the infant congregation said: "Blessed is he who forsakes his father and his mother for my sake. Those that hear my words are my father and my mother" (Achebe, TFA 139).

In *Arrow of God*, Ezeulu scrutinizes the emerging realities with vision and insight. He is acutely aware of the bitter truth that the white man had not come for a short visit, but to build a house and live, and there was no escape for them. The white man had not only brought a religion, but also a government to protect the followers of their religion. They had built a court where the District Commissioner judged cases, which were brought by the court messengers. The District Officers preferred the local Africans in their own district, as their rustic way of life offered little threat to their status.

It was easy for them to deal with the unsophisticated peasants whose main concern was to earn their livelihood, that to, keeping in peace with the neighbours. For them, to manage the urban educated mass was difficult as they resented their paternalistic system. They were more interested in the political growth of their country, and the eventual attainment of its independence.

Fig 11. ***The good shepherd*: District Administrative Officer from Trevor Royle, *Winds of Change* (London: John Murray, 1996) N.pag.**

In *Things Fall Apart,* the court messengers were greatly hated in Umuofia as they were foreigners, and arrogant and high-handed. When Umuofia pays a fine of two hundred and 50 bags of cowries, to release his six men, the extra fifty bags eventually went into the hands of the court messengers. The six leaders of Umuofia, including Okonkwo, were treated with utter disregard, irrespective of their status. It speaks volumes of the colonial arrogance, so deep-rooted in the colonizer's sensibility. The leaders were badly beaten to leave wound marks on their bodies.

Achebe presents the white man as quite clever and intelligent, who used the Igbos against their own people. They allured and tempted the deserving men from the society to act as Warrant Chiefs for different villages. Though Ezeulu of *Arrow of God* refused to accept the post of Warrant Chief, there were many others who accepted the offer, and later exploited their own people. Achebe accepts the fact that Igboland was deprived of true and honest leaders, which did not let Nigeria grow and develop:

> The lack of real leaders in Igboland goes back, of course, to the beginnings of colonial administration. Once the white man had crushed Igbo resistance it was relatively easy for him to locate upstarts and ruffians in the community who would uphold his regime at the expense of their own people. From those days the average Igbo leader's mentality has not been entirely free of the collaborating Warrant Chief syndrome (Achebe, *The Trouble with Nigeria* 48).

The new religion brought by the white man was a miracle which gave the Igbos a lot of tolerance towards the outcasts or osus who were given entry into the church. An osu was a slave to one of the many gods of the clan. He was a 'thing set apart', despised and discarded by the society. Osus who had carried with them the mark of the forbidden caste—the long, tangled, and dirty hair; shaved off their hair, and soon were among the strongest adherents of the new faith. The white man also welcomed the twins which were an abomination, and so thrown into the bad bush. The change upcoming in the Igbo society was thus described by one of the oldest members of the Umunna:

> A man can now leave his father and his brothers. He can curse the gods of his fathers and his ancestors, like a hunter's dog that suddenly goes mad and turns to his master. I fear for you; I fear for the clan (Achebe, TFA 152).

Anarchy could be seen in the Igbo society where their own men and sons joined the ranks of the stranger, and helped to uphold their government. The converts grappled to develop the relationship between the new faith, their cultural inheritance, and the needs and obligation of their immediate environment. The missionaries were quite clever to get the converts largely from the poor categories, or from those suffering from some abnormalities. So it was basically the peasants, ex-slaves, the widows, the osus, and the childless who got attracted to the New Religion. As they were offered bribe, in cash or in kind, they could not say 'no' to Christianity. But by the time the realisation dawns on the elders, it is too late for them to realize their own mistakes. In *Things Fall Apart,* Obierika shares his concern with Okonkwo:

> He [white man] has won our brothers, and our clan can no longer act like one. He has put a knife on the things that held us together and we have fallen apart (Achebe 160).

In *Arrow of God* (AOG), Chinua has shown the positive thinking of the character, 'Ezeulu' who sends his son Oduche to learn the ways of white man, in order to understand their culture and traditions. Like the elder Nweka Ukpaka, he understands the need to combat the alien culture strategically and tactfully as "The white man is like a hot soup and we [they] must take him slowly-slowly from the edges of the bowl" (AOG 85). But later, the new religion creates adverse circumstances for Ezeulu which results in his downfall. The new religion said, "Leave you yam, leave your cocoyam and come to church" (43). The white man did adopt the policy of divide and rule, and took advantage of the dispute among the clans. The white man sat in judgement over Umuaro and Okperi, and gave the disputed land to Okperi. They had indeed created a situation where things were 'falling apart'. The new religion could instigate the people to go against their age-old customs. In *Arrow of God,* Mr. Good country told the converts of Umuaro that they should be ready to kill the python just as the people of the rivers had killed iguana. He asked them to not to forget that python was a snake who had deceived their first mother—Eve. He blackmailed them by saying that if they did not kill it, they should not count themselves a Christian. In *Arrow of God,* Oduche internalizes the new custom, and kills the python which was sacred to the Ibo clan, as the christians said that it was savage and heathen. Achebe reflects such examples to show what colonization does to the various cultural, spiritual, and intellectual foundations of Ibo cohesion:

> Directly or indirectly, the British have "imprisoned" the guns of Umuaro, the sacred python, the keeper of cyclic time,

> and the yams that symbolize both the political power of the people and their spiritual well-being (Barthold, *Black Time Fiction* 149).

In *Arrow of God,* the market place and the day of Eke, are the iconography of the Ibo people which was changed into Eke Okperi market, the biggest market, as the white man took his merchandise there. This act by them allows the reader to evaluate the problem of change in the cultural values and ideology of the Ibo, as a result of the participation and imposition of the British. Within the confines of colonial impact is the land ownership question, another problem presented by Achebe in *Arrow of God.* The white man came and made the Igbo think that the land was theirs, and they had full authority to sort out the disputes related to it.

In his book of essays *Home and Exile,* Achebe corelates the title 'Education' with formal education at School, at Sunday School, and in Church. He describes the atmosphere of the school which was always tense. Achebe asserts that they were lucky if a day passed without receiving a stroke or two of the teachers' cane. He was pained to acquire education as it was not about Igbo things; it was only about far-away places and peoples. He relates the establishment of schools that breed a new indigenous leadership, the trading stores that create a new economic elite, and a new power structure that relegated the old titled class to the background. Harry Franklin, Incharge of the Department of Public Information in Northern Rhodesia noted approvingly:

> I learnt that Africans were no longer almost exclusively interested in local and tribal affairs. They wanted to read and hear more about other parts of the territory, other countries in Africa and in Europe. Something new was stirring in their minds and hearts. Their letters sometimes referred to 'living in a new environment', to 'waking up', to 'the modern world' (Royle, *Winds of Change* 108).

In *No Longer at Ease,* Chinua has presented the aspirations of the Igbo people from the youth. They were aware of the growth which they expected of their society, and which they knew was impossible without the European education. The oldest man in the meeting of Umuofia Progressive Union said:

> Many towns have four or five or even ten of their sons in European posts in this city. Umuofia has only one. And now our enemies say that even one is too many for us. But our ancestors will not agree to such a thing (Achebe, *No Longer at Ease* 7).

The life and career of Obi Okonkwo in *No Longer at Ease* prove that the advent of white civilization let looser a 'blood-dimmed' tide of anarchy on African life. The European education had changed his outlook towards life and society. His faith in the Igbo culture is lost, and he adopts the new culture. By this time, the people had accepted the strength and power of the white man. For them, to throw a white man was like unmasking an ancestral spirit. In this novel, Chinua Achebe tries to defend Africa. His respect for his country is quite obvious, as he ridicules the white man sarcastically:

> It was clear he [Mr. Green] loved Africa, but only Africa of a kind: the Africa of Charles, the messenger, the Africa of his gardenboy and steward boy. He must have come originally with an ideal—to bring light to the heart of darkness, to tribal headhunters performing weird ceremonies and unspeakable rites. But ..., Africa played him false (Achebe 121).

In *A Man of the People* (MOP), Chinua depicts the postcolonial impact on the Nigerian clans. Chief Nanga, a corrupt politician, fought against the white man who were corrupt, and now Nanga was eating the reward of his courage. In this novel, the interference of Britishers and Americans even after independence can be seen. The British amalgamated paid 400 thousand pounds to P.O.PO to fight the election, and American had even paid more. Mr. John, a young American can be seen boasting:

> America may not be perfect..., but don't forget that we are the only powerful country in the entire history of the world, the only one, which had the power to conquer others and didn't do it. (Achebe, MOP 45).

It seems that Chinua wants to show that the Nigerian clans had surrendered themselves to the fate. Corruption and treachery had become a part of their culture and tradition. People's opinion about the leaders was that, "Let them eat..., after all when white men used to do all the eating did we commit suicide? Of course not" (MOP 145). In "Marriage is a Private Affair" in *Girls at War,* Achebe shows the impact of colonialism in the life of the Igbos even with regard to marriage. Achebe has shown Lagos as modern, where as, those living in the remote areas as orthodox, and under the influence of the new 'Culture' and the new 'Religion'. Nnaemeka tells to his wife Nene that the elders of the village were most unhappy if the engagement was not arranged by them. Nnaemeka's father writes to him from the distant village:

> I have found a girl who will suit you admirably…She has a proper Christian upbringing...Her Sunday School teacher has told me that she reads her Bible very fluently (Achebe, *Girls at War* 24).

Achebe has been successful in showing in painful detail, the struggle between the British colonial administration and his protagonists. He narrates the social and historical conditions of African society before and during colonialism. Achebe admits that though Igbos accepted Christian beliefs, they were not fanatical. Their lives were ruled, as much by reason as by faith; as much by common sense and compassion as by doctrine. Though Achebe brings up many important issues on African colonialism, his novels and short stories have not attracted much attention of the critics.

Works Cited

Achebe, Chinua. *A Man of the People.* New York: Ancho.

______________ *Arrow of God.* New York: Anchor, 1974.

______________ *Girls at War and other Stories.* New York: Anchor, 1973.

______________ *Home and Exile.* New York: Anchor, 2000.

______________ *Hopes and Impediments: Selected Essays.* New York: Anchor, 1988.

______________ *No Longer at Ease.* New York: Anchor.

______________ *The Trouble with Nigeria.* London: Heinemann, 1983.

______________ *Things Fall Apart.* New Delhi: Allied, 2004.

Barthold, Bonnie. J. *Black Time Fiction of Africa, the Caribbean and the United* States. New Haven: Conn:. Yale Univ. Press, 1981.

"Embodiment in African Literature." *English Essays.* 2004 http : // www. englishessays.org.uk/english_essays/embodiment_african_literature.php.

February, V.A. *Mind Your Colour: The 'coloured' Stereotype in South African Literature*. London: Kegan Paul, 1981.

Gathering Seaweed: African Prison Writing. Ed.Jack Mapanje. London: Heinemann, 2002.

Isichei, Elizabeth. *A History of Christianity in Africa: From Antiquity to the present*. London: Cromwell, 1995.

Royle, Trevor. *Winds of Change: The End of Empire in Africa*. London: John Murray, 1966.

5 Whirlpool of Change

Achebe, in his novels, talks of the story of Africa in the modern world and its problem with Europe. He views Africa from different angle and feels that Africa is the masquerade which has to be viewed from different perspectives. As he feels that there is seminal relationship between art and society, and an artist and audience, his terms involve commitment to social causes. He draws upon the colourful Mbari ceremony of the Oweri Igbo as an example of aesthetics where collectivity is accorded importance rather than individual expression of creativity. He is of the opinion that art belongs to all, and is a 'function' of society. He presents the problem of evolution and the helplessness of Ibo people to accept the British will. He shows the change in the Ibo society due to the intrusion of British Colonialism and Christianity.

Apart from fiction, Achebe also wrote a collection of essays, short stories, and poems. His works can be summarised into two sets—Fiction and Non-fiction.

A. Fiction

Achebe's *Things Fall Apart* (1958), portrays tribal Africa, particularly the Ibo society of the second half of the nineteenth century. It was the time when Britain was in the process of colonizing not only Igboland but also other African territories. His novel got its title from W.B. Yeats' poem, "The Second Coming":

> Turning and turning in the widening gyre
> The falcon cannot hear the falconer;
> Things fall apart; the center cannot hold;
> Mere anarchy is loosed upon the world
>
> (*The Faber Book* 58)

Fig 12. ***Things Fall Apart*****, a fiction**

Source: Electronic

Achebe loved Irishman's beautiful poems and found the phrase "things fall apart" quite apt and appropriate for his novel. He wrote *Things Fall Apart* (TFA) as a response to Joyce Cary's *Mr. Johnson*. He says that the novels' fundamental theme is that the African people did not hear of culture for the first time from Europeans. Therefore, *Things Fall Apart* celebrates tribal society in all its value, depth, and beauty. This novel is a representation of the dignity that African people mostly lost, during the colonial period, when white settlers entered the country. It analyses the destruction of the bond between individuals and society, with the destruction of the African culture.

Chinua's novels *Things Fall Apart* and *Arrow of God*, focus on Nigeria's early experience with colonialism, from first contact with the British to widespread British administration. The former tells the story of the Ibo village of the late 1800s and the trials and tribulations of Okonkwo, a tragic hero. In Igboland, Okonkwo means a man born on *nkwo* day, i.e., the first day of the Igbo week.

The Ibo tribe, in which Okonkwo was a leader, can be seen as representative of all indigenous peoples worldwide who came face-to-face with British invasive tactics. Okonkwo, popularly known as 'Roaring Flame', is presented by Achebe as a champion wrestler, a wealthy farmer, a husband to three wives, a title-holder among his people, and a member of the select egwugwu whose members impersonate ancestral spirits at tribal rituals. His whole life is dominated by fear, fear of failure and weakness. and a need to escape the shame of his father's failure. As he loathes his father, he instinctively hates everything that reminds him of Unoka. As Unoka is weak, Okonkwo strives at all times to exhibit heroic courage, which pushes him to commit excesses:

> As the man who had cleared his throat drew up and raised his matchet, Okonkwo looked away. He heard the blow. The pot fell and broke in the sand. He heard Ikemefuna cry, "My father; they have killed me!" as he ran towards him. Dazed with fear, Okonkwo drew his matchet and cut him down. He was afraid of being thought weak (Achebe, TFA 55).

Since Okonkwo takes extremist positions in life, he is unable to balance in assessment of the situations. For him, the white institutions must be destroyed not simply because they are exotic, but more urgently because they are decided obstacles to his own upward movement. To him, the new colonial dispensation is an unmitigated evil that should be effaced from his home. But many men and women in Umuofia view it differently. They get attracted by the developments taking place in their society. They know that Christianity is being imposed upon them. They can realize that the new religion is a lunatic one which can replace their traditional one. But they can visualize some changes which can benefit their society. For the first time, palm oil and kernel have become the things of great price and much money flows into Umuofia. That is the reason they do not want to protest the white man. This difference in perception relates to the problem why Umofia does not join Okonkwo in a battle to drive out the new colonial administration and the Christian missionaries. Okonkwo's real suffering begins when his gun not only fires accidently, but kills a clansman, Ezeudu's son, he being the oldest man in that quarter of Umuofia:

> The seven years of exile that follow are, literally, seven years of estrangement from the passage of time in Umuofia. Okonkwo sees his exile within the perspective of cyclic recurrence: when he has expiated his crime, he will return to Umuofia and take up where he left off seven years before. In Eliade's terms, he confers a "cyclic direction upon time, annuls its irreversibility. Everything begins over again....No event is irreversible and no transformation is final" (qtd.in Barthold, *Black Time Fiction* 59).

Okonkwo has not anticipated any change in Umuofia while he is in exile. He wants time to stop for him so that he can get what all he possessed—his titles, his position and the respect which he has in society. But the appearance of the white man in Africa which has brought an alien and a more powerful culture has caused the traditional society to fall apart. Umuofia is no longer an isolated, bracketed world. It has become a new world where the colonizer, his culture and values have influenced every level of existence. He is unable to accept the changes taking place in his society and so becomes helpless and dejected. He laments upon his homecoming, "Perhaps I have been away too long...What is it that has happened to our people?" (TFA 159). In the end, in frustration, he kills an African employed by the British, and then commits suicide, a sin against the tradition to which he had long clung. His dream to dictate the society seduces him away from Umuofian tradition, and when he dies, he is so far removed from the mainstream of Umuofian life that he could be said to represent little more than himself. In the novel's final paragraph, the commissioner muses about how he would describe Okonkwo's suicide in his memoirs, 'The Pacification of the Primitive Tribes of the Lower Niger.' In *Things Fall Apart*, 'Things' symbolize culture, traditions, customs, rituals, and ceremonies of the Africans. 'Things' characterize brittleness, which can easily be broken or snapped. Likewise though the Igbos had deep-rooted beliefs and customs, the Europeans could change their beliefs and shatter their dreams and aspirations. Achebe makes the readers realize the pain and agony which one feels on losing all of one's possessions.

Achebe's second novel *No Longer at Ease,* was published in 1960, which is a sequel of *Things Fall Apart*. It took its title from T.S. Eliot's poem, "Journey of the Magi" in which Eliot says:

> We returned to our places, these kingdoms,
> But no longer at ease here, in the old dispensation,
> With an alien people clutching their gods.
> I should be glad of another death (*The Faber Book* 105).

Fig 13. *No Longer at Ease,* a fiction

This novel revolves around Obi Okonkwo. Obi, the grandson of Okonkwo of *Things Fall Apart,* and son of Nwoye, was the Christian convert and catechist christened as Issac. Obi, a young man of education and promise, returns from England to construct a better and healthier Nigeria. He is firmly determined to create a new nation and a better social order and join the Senior Civil Service with a belief that, "...the public service of Nigeria would remain corrupt until the old Africans at the top were replaced by young men from the universities" (44).

When Obi lands there, he finds that Nigeria is no longer a land of his dreams. He ponders over ill-advised traditions such as paying bride price, the *osu* practice and newly ushered in material values like the English Education, and the western way of life. Obi, though a sensible young man, falls prey to the circumstances, and becomes a corrupt man. The Umuofia Progressive Union, in Umuofia, which is the hometown of Obi, discuss in a gathering:

> We paid eight hundred pounds to train him in England...But instead of being grateful he insults us because of a useless girl (Achebe, *No Longer at Ease* 5).

Obi is given scholarship under a scheme in which all the people of Umuofia, an Ibo village in Eastern Nigeria, have contributed their hard-earned money to accumulate eight hundred pounds which Obi has to repay within four years of his return from England. The villagers sacrifice thinking that in future Obi would be able to sort out all the landcases against their neighbours. But instead of law, he reads English. When he returns to Lagos, he is amazed to see the changed scenario. Lagos was associated with electric lights, motor cars and brightly dressed girls. There was no darkness there because of the electric lights which shone at night. Much developments had taken place in Lagos. The people who did not prefer walking could wave their hand to stop the pleasure car. Obi's friend, Joseph, had much to tell Obi about Lagos—about the cinema and the dance halls and about political meetings—about a strange and sinful new world. When Obi was in England, he really seem to miss Nigeria, the Igbo food and the Igbo people. He remembered his country for its scenic beauty and simplicity. During first winter in England, Obi had written a nostalgic poem about Nigeria which shows his love for motherland:

> How sweet it is to lie beneath a tree
> At eventime and share the ecstasy
> Of jocund birds and flimsy butterflies;
> How sweet to leave our earthbound body in its mud,
> And rise towards the music of the spheres,
> Descending softly with the wind,
> And the tender glow of the fading sun
>
> (Achebe, *No Longer at Ease* 19).

Achebe presents Obi as a sensible young man who could question the unjust authority of Mr. Green, his English boss. He could also thwart the practice of accepting bribe in personal life and was not affected by false pride. But Obi fails due to his indecisiveness, as he was like his grandfather Okonkwo of *Things Fall Apart*. He experiences an arduous struggle, both in his domestic front as well as professional, which leads him to the temporal chaos. As a child, he was not allowed by his father to have any association with the "heathens" in his village. And as a youth when he is rejected by the traditional world of his grandfather, he is totally shattered. Obi finds himself changed in the noisy, crowded streets of Lagos. The sacrifice of the Igbo village appears to be simply a loan to him. Obi who occupied a European post in the civil service and earned nearly fifty pounds a month, becomes reluctant to pay twenty pounds a month, as a part of repayment of his loans to the Progressive Union. Obi tends to be an offshoot of a weak, hybrid culture:

> That is what Lagos can do to a young man. He runs after sweet things, dances breast to breast with women and forgets his home and his people (Achebe, *No Longer at Ease* 181).

Obi got influenced by the culture of Lagos. But he also could realize that they had not reached the stage where he could ignore all his customs and marry Clara, an *osu* or an outcast. Obi's ideals start disintegrating when Clara vehemently disapproves of her marriage with him, she being an *osu* girl. Obi becomes a prey to emotional turmoil and loses his moral balance. Neither he could retain faith in the old norms and values, nor he could conform to the ideas of the west. He represents the common struggle of educated Africans who stood confounded between acceptance and rejection.

Achebe presents in the novel a brilliant description and analysis of the situations and conflicts. He shows the innocent thoughts of the people of Ibo village even amidst crisis. The President of the Umuofia Progressive Union shares his viewpoint in a gathering which was in favour of Obi. He expresses his trust on Obi saying that England could not change his blood. And that he would always stand for his people, as he was like a bird that flew off the earth, but landed on an anthill, thereby showing that he was still on the ground. But Obi proved him to be wrong as he had become corrupt. His spirit had died, he did not feel like visiting his hometown, Umuofia, even when his mother had expired. He got used to the system of bribe prevalent in Lagos and gets caught red-handed accepting bribe. Sleeping with a girl was no longer a bribery for him. The life and career of Obi prove that the advent of white civilization brought about anarchy on African life:

> Obi's situation symbolizes the plight of the new generation of Africans—exposed to Western culture and education at conflict with traditional values and ideals—who painfully discover the persistence of tradition and the shifting notions, wrongly conceived and perceived, as a result of the strong demands of tradition. They are hopelessly caught in the throes of tradition
>
> (qtd.in Singh, *Rethinking Colonialism* 71).

Achebe makes an attempt to show that one should aspire for a better living and comforts, but not at the cost of one's self-esteem. Obi did a blunder by not trusting his own people, he being under the influence of the aliens, the white man—their culture and beliefs. He becomes a stranger in his own country, with no emotions and sentiments for his people.

Set in a time frame between *Things Fall Apart* and *No Longer at Ease*, Achebe's third novel *Arrow of God*, (1964) reveals the impact of colonialism on African society. In this novel, Achebe relates to three key players who disrupt the indigenous society of Umuaro. First, there is a priest-king, who is invested with a tremendous power to be exercised in the interest of his people. Second, there is the colonial administrator Winterbottom, servant of the Brittanic majesty, who acts as a broker between the imperial will and the welfare of his people. Finally, there is the Christian missionary enterprise that works as a middle ground between the priest of the Igbo society and the colonial administration.

In *Arrow of God* (AOG), six villages—Umuachala, Umunneora, Umuagu, Umuezeani, Umugwugwa and Umaisiuzo took the name of Umuaro, and the priest of Ulu, Ezeulu, became their Chief Priest.

He became the mediator between the people and their god. Achebe seems to show that though 'U' was common in the six villages, before Ezeulu became the Priest, there was no 'Unity' among them. They lived as different people, and each worshipped its own deity. Their lives were not secured as the hired soldiers of Abame used to strike in the dead of night, set fire to the houses carry men, women and children into slavery. So now it was their god-Ezeulu, the priest of Ulu which had become symbolic of 'Unity':

> Threatened with destruction by a hostile community, six villages unite for the sake of their survival, the mode of their unification making it clear that effective warfare and spiritual unity are inseparable as they unite under the aegis of a single deity (Barthold, *Black Time Fiction* 140).

Fig 14. ***Arrow of God*, a fiction**

Ezeulu thought that he had immense power over the year, over the crops and therefore over the people. He has been described as "half spirit" and "half human" who in his ritual appearances carried in his right hand "Nne Ofo", the mother of all staffs of authority in Umuaro. No doubt, he named the day for the feast of Pumpkin leaves and the New Yam Feast, but did not choose it. He could refuse no festival, no planting, no reaping, and so was merely a "watchman", his power being that of a child over a goat. Ezeulu, firstly, sends his son Oduche to join the white to know about their ways and keep an eye on their actions. But instead of becoming a spy, he becomes a convert. And then Ezeulu is bewildered by the ways of the new age. He could see the society changing. He regarded himself to be the god who founded their town. That is the reason why, when he hears of Umuaro having taken war to Okperi, he feels shocked. He could not expect the people to take their own decisions. He felt that Umuaro had become too wise in its own conceit, like the little bird, nza, who ate and drank, and challenged his personal god to single combat. Ezeulu's only fault was that he expected everyone—his wives, his kinsmen, his children, his friends, and even his enemies to think and act like himself. Anyone who dared to say 'no' to him was an enemy. In his thoughts, he rebels against the notion that he was merely an arrow in the hands of God. Ezeulu was stung to anger if any of his enemy challenged his potential. Ezeulu had become so egotist that he could not listen a negative reply from anyone. He became so confident of his power that he did not expect any one to stand against him. But time did not favour him for long. The people of Umuaro could realize that the aspirations of Ezeulu could lead them nowhere. So they stood against him. Nwaka, of Umunneora, told the assembly that Umuaro must not allow itself to be led by the Chief Priest of Ulu:

> Ezeulu is a man of ambition; he wants to be king, priest, diviner, all. His father, they said, was like that too. But Umuaro showed him that Igbo people knew no kings.The time has come to tell his son also (Achebe, *Arrow of God* 27).

Ezeulu becomes a 'tool' or an 'arrow' in the bow of his God with no power in his own hands. Captain Winterbottom, a typical colonial officer, sends messengers to Umuaro to fetch Ezeulu as it was planned to give warrant of office to Ezeulu in the presence of the *ndichie* or elders of his clan. On Ezeulu's refusal, he is imprisoned in Okperi. He temporarily loses his status as Chief Priest which is very painful for him.The elders of Umuaro felt that his condition was like the puppy in the proverb which attempted to answer too calls at once and broke its jaw. Five years ago, Ezeulu had asked the villagers to not to defy the white man as they were very powerful. But the people had taken arms which were broken by them across their knees. And now Ezeulu wanted to go against the white man when his people had learnt to accept the changes taking place in society. As the priest of Ulu , he was the keeper of Time. Achebe shows the inability of Ezeulu to keep pace with the time and announce the New Yam Festival resulting in famine. Ezeulu refuses to call the harvest when the yams are ripe in the field, and explains to the elders of Umuaro:

> ...You all know what our custom is. I only call a new festival when there is only one yam left from the last. Today I have three yams and so I know that the time has not come (AOG 207).

The plight of Umuaro lay more heavily on Ezeulu and his family than other people knew. With every passing day, Umuaro became more and more an alien silence—the kind of silence which burnt a man's inside like the blue, quiet, razor-edge flame of burning palmnut shells. White man taking advantage of the situation invited the villages to offer their left over yams, to sacrifice it to their 'God' in the church. So the British could invade Umuaro not with the help of their soldiers but with help of their 'God'. The sacrificial yams which was a proud thing in the past, became a shameful act eschewed by the elders:

> The meaning of sacrifice is reduced to something like an individual business transaction, a "payment" for survival, and Christianity is thus portrayed as a "social organization...demanding payment for the symbols of membership" (qtd. in Barthold, *Black Time Fiction* 148).

Chinua Achebe's *Arrow of God*, shows that no man, however great, is greater than his people. The God had taken sides with Umuaro and its leaders against their headstrong and ambitious priest. But Ulu had chosen a dangerous time to uphold their decision.Their motive to destroy their priest brought about disaster for them as well. It gave the people a liberty to accept the 'new religion and the 'new god'. As Ezeulu did not call for the harvest, the missionaries got a chance to call for the harvest. They invited the people to send their sons with a yam or two to offer to the new religion so that the harvest could take place without the wrath of Ulu. The Christian harvest which took place after a few days, saw more people than even Good country [one of the missionaries] dreamed. Ezeulu's condition was not better than the rat who could not flee fast and so made way for the tortoise to win the battle. For Ezeulu it was as though he had died. In this novel, Achebe has tried to show the connectivity in between illiteracy and ignorance. To be simple and innocent is one thing, to be ignorant is another. The Igbos were simple and illiterate, but ignorant as well. They could not foresee the intentions of the white man. They wanted to gain education, and to grow and to prosper at the cost of their freedom. Igbos were tempted by the change—the change in culture, the change in religion, and the change in beliefs. The change came, but at a very high cost.

Published in 1966, Achebe's fourth novel, *A Man of the People,* attempts to grapple with the postcolonial realities. In this novel, Achebe ridicules the corrupt leaders of Nigeria. On one side is Odili Samalu, the narrator— a university graduate and a high school teacher with an honest desire to promote the common good. On the other, is Chief, the Honourable M.N. Nanga—a parliamentarian and cabinet minister, the most amoral politician dedicated to reap the utmost personal gain from his position. He was nicknamed as M.A. Minus Opportunity.

Achebe says: "Whether you asked in the city or in his home village, Anata, they would tell you he was a man of the people" (*A Man of the people* 1).

Achebe ridicules the silly and ignorant villagers who were dancing themselves lame, waiting to blow off their gunpowder in honour of the minister M.A. Nanga, he who had moved the country down the slopes of inflation. The villagers accepted the corrupt politician as normal and sensible being who did not spit out the juicy morsel that good fortune had placed in his mouth Odili Samalu comes to the capital to take a strategic post in the civil service. He even wished to go to Europe but stooping for scholarship was next to impossible for him. But ill-fate took Odili to Chief Nanga. Admiring the grand exquisite suite and the comforts of "seven bedrooms and seven bathrooms" in the minister's official residence, Odili is struck by the luxury. He then wishes to be a minister for ever. At this juncture, "Achebe skillfully moves from the political to the personal" (qtd.in Singh, *Rethinking Colonialsm* 148). Mr. Nanga, a man of fifty, having a son and a wife , wrenched Odili's girlfriend Elsie from his hand and led her to bed under Odili's very eyes. Odili could do nothing as Mr. Nanga was a Minister, wealthy with a lot of public money, riding in a Cadillac and watched over by a one- eyed hired thug.

Fig 15. *A Man of the People,* a fiction

Odili plans a revenge from Mr. Nanga by misguiding his would-be parlour wife Edna, but falls in love with her. He forms a new party C.P.C. with Max and his friends, to form a new era of cleanliness in the politics of Nigeria. For Odili, all things seemed so mixed up; his revenge, his new political ambition, and the girl. Nanga then tries to persuade Odili to leave the national politics to those like himself. He even tempts him with the offer of a scholarship for advanced study abroad. But when is unable to convince the young man, Nanga let loose his thugs, who beat Odili to within an inch of his life. When anarchy erupts in between the thugs of the rival parties, the Prime Minister unilaterally appoints his old cabinet. But as the turmoil still existed, the army stages a coup and throws the leaders in jail. At the end, Achebe's novel *A Man of the People* ends with a positive note: "The fat-dripping, gummy, eat-and-let-eat regime just ended...You chop, me self I chop, palaver finish"(149). Achebe condemns the people, who owned a thousand names of adulation for the politicians, within a single night, criticised the last regime—its oppression and corruption. Killiam has made the interesting observation that "Odili is the man Obi [No Longer at Ease] might have become" (qtd. in Ed. Okpewho, *A CaseBook* 17). Achebe's novel conveys the message to the amoral leaders that their rule would be short-lived if they do not change their attitude towards the people. Leaders are actually 'Men' who are supposed to work for the society. So if the leaders do not fulfil their responsibility, they are destined to be discarded by the people who supported them earlier.

After a long gestation period of 20 years Achebe's fifth novel *Anthills of the Savannah,* a post colonial fiction, was published in 1988. The title of the novel comes from a proverb about "anthills surviving to tell the new grass of the Savannah about last years bush fires", underlining the usefulness of the narrative tradition in bearing the seeds of future renewal. Achebe exposes the readers to a much wider theatre of experience in Nigerian and global politics and culture. He considers the civil war in Biafran war, as one of the reasons which virtually changed the history of Nigeria. This novel shows all aspects of colonial process from the beginning to the end of the colonial contact. It tells the story of three schoolmates, Ikem, Chris, and Sam, who became figures in a new regime in the fictional West African Land of Kangan. Chris strives to make a commitment to his fellow citizens. Ikem who comes from an elite class makes his wisdom available to a wider spectrum of the population. Chris's fiancée, Beatrice also plays a prominent role as an equal partner with males in the quest for change and a new social order. Achebe addresses the course, unbridled power often takes and demonstrates how pursuit of self-interest comes at tremendous cost to the community as a whole. He talks in detail about the kind of people who are involved in leadership, and the kind of education which the people need to acquire in order to be fit for the tasks. This novel brings forth the aspirations of the educated youth who wish to see rapid changes in their society. They do realize later that its their own culture and tradition which can lead to reforms, and form a new social order. In his interview with Chris Searle, Achebe says that:

> Our leaders do not realize how quickly they become completely cut off. It doesn't take a year! You move in cars with sirens and everybody clears the route for you—they even pave the road for you before you make a visit...And if you are not careful you quickly lose touch (*Writing Across Worlds* 60).

Achebe portrays women in his fictional universe in the existing socio-cultural situation of the period he is depicting, and also the male attitude towards women. He describes the source, nature, and extent of female subordination, and oppression in Nigerian society. Writers such as Ama Ata Aidoo of Ghana and the late Flora Nwapa of Nigeria has insisted that the image of the helpless, dependent, unproductive African woman was one ushered in by European imperialists whose women lived that way. But Rose U. Mezu feels that Nigeria's traditional culture, Muslim as well as non-Muslim, had been masculine-based even before the advent of the white man. The colonial rule merely aggravated the situation by introducing a lopsided system in which African men received a well-rounded education, while the African women received only utilitarian skills to help the educated men.

Achebe opens before us a world in which patriarchy intrudes oppressively into every sphere of existence. The world in *Things Fall Apart* is andocentric where the man is everything and the woman nothing. In domestic terms, women are quantified as part of men's acquisition. One was a successful farmer, warrior, and a man of worth if one had three wives, yam barns and social titles. In TFA, Nwakibie was rich as he had three huge barns, nine wives, and 30 children, and the highest but one title which a man can take in the clan. Achebe explains that, "Yam stood for manliness, and he who could feed his family on yams from one harvest to another was a very great man indeed" (30). To produce an abundant harvest, the traditional farmer needed a good work force and so women became the core of the rural workforce—farming, tending animals, nurturing children, among other activities. Achebe's novels clearly show that the woman's place was in the home. They were ignored, exploited, degenerated, and made to feel as inferiors. They were not allowed to stay in any discussion, were excluded in the councils of war, and were not a part of the masquerades representing the judiciary and the ancestral spirits. Achebe also shows the change in the status of women in Igbo society due to the coming of white man who used Christianity as their weapon. The new religion accepted the outcasts or the weak women who were designed to be rejected and discarded by the African society. Achebe's works confirm the development and progression of Igbo women with the increase in urbanization and modernization. The women no longer remained within the four walls, and accepted the challenges in the modern Igbo society. Their decisions might have brought happiness or sadness in their lives, but atleast it was their decision based on their free will. Achebe convinces the readers that African women can be the partners with men in national progress and development, and can gain individual self-realisation and fulfilment.

Achebe's *Girls at War* and other Short Stories (1973), contain a story titled "The Madman" where the reader is taken through the post colonial effects on the character Nwibe which makes him mad. He experiences an internal cultural conflict which makes him lose his senses. When a madman steals Nwibe's cloth, while the latter is bathing, and the naked citizen chases the now-clothed madman, the town people judge incorrectly. They assume Nwibe who is naked, as the mad one. The family consults two medicine men: one says Nwibe cannot be treated; the other, less famous and less strict, agrees to attempt a cure. Nwibe is cured, and the town people praise the successful medicine man. Achebe seems to symbolize the stealing of Nwibe's cloth with the loss of culture. With the coming of the white man, the Africans had lost their culture and identity. Nwibe reflects the condition of every African who drove mad under the colonial impact, and which made them lose their self-esteem.

Fig 16. *Anthills of the Savannah,* a fiction

B. Non-fiction

Chinua's short story "Chike's School Days" in *Girls at War* clearly shows the impact of colonialism on the Igbo tribe. Chike, who was the son of an *osu* women—an outcaste, looks down upon the heathens of the village. It was because Chike was brought up in the ways of the white man. He liked hymn-singing in the morning and at night. At the village school, he loved singing songs in English from the *Chambers' Dictionary*. Thus for Chike, the world of the white man, was like a strange, magical new world which gave him bliss and happiness. It was the English Education that created a rift among the Africans. Even a school-going child—Chike, could feel himself superior under the influence of the white man. Thus it was a feeling of inferiority in the blacks which made them imbibe the Western culture.

Fig 17. ***Girls at War,*** **a fiction**

Achebe's another story "The Sacrificial Egg" in *Girls at War* depicts the all-powerful European trading company which brought palm-kernels, cloth, and metalware from the Igbos at its own price. Julius Obi worked as a clerk in the offices of this company in the village of Umuru. The village was scared of 'Kitikpa', the incarnate power of smallpox, which demanded the sacrifice of the inhabitants who owed to the Gods of the soil. Achebe shows the dread of the villagers who did not move out in the streets for the fear that they might meet 'Kitikpa' on the streets. But when Julius was out one night, he stepped on an egg offered in sacrifice and is oppressed by misfortune:

> It was barely a week ago but already it seemed like another life, separated from the present by a vast emptiness. This emptiness deepened with every passing day. On this side of it stood Julius, and on the other Ma and Janet whom the dread artist decorated (Achebe, *Girls at War* 48-49).

In "The Sacrifical Egg", Achebe wants to show the impact of the schools and the churches on the youth, who were behaving no better than the strangers. The Igbos were captivated by the new religion, which demanded sacrifice of their primitive beliefs and customs. Julius has been shown to suffer, as he is a part of the new culture, and is a clerk in the European offices. The stepping on a Sacrificial Egg was something which was against the Igbos' rituals. They have been shown as helpless, with no power in hand to drive away the Europeans. It was only the disease—smallpox, which could make the white man leave their village.

In 1983, in Nigeria, Achebe wrote a little political book out of some desperation before the elections called *The Trouble with Nigeria*. He was concerned with the question of leadership and felt that the main problem in Nigeria was lack of true leadership, and the widespread corruption. No doubt, he points to few great leaders like the late Aminu Kano, who held high offices, but still came out to be a very poor man. Achebe also gives the example of Julius Nyerere, a legendary figure, who was not corrupt and dishonest. So for Achebe, a true leader is one who does not fall prey to greed and corruption. He talks openly about the climate of Nigeria which is of indiscipline. Achebe feels that there can be no better place to observe the thrusting indiscipline in Nigerian behaviour than on the roads:

> As the climate of indiscipline settles firmly on the land, the reasonable driver who stays in line begins to look more and more like a dummy, a naive fool who may be doing what the book says but will get nowhere at all because "this is not Britain or America but Nigeria"
>
> (*The Trouble with Nigeria* 29).

Achebe has proved himself to be an honest writer. He is quite sincere in revealing the problems which are the common features of Nigeria. He accepts that they have false image of themselves, and have much scope for development. He asserts that the Igbos will have to struggle hard to make Nigeria a better place to live.

Chinua's book, *Hopes and Impediments* (1988), is a brilliant collection of essays which encourages the readers to think past their stubborn preconceptions. In his famous essay "An Image of Africa", he talks of the Racism in Conrad's *Heart of Darkness*. He sarcastically comments on Conrad's book which he feels has been notoriously inaccurate in rendering about African history. He feels that an author should not be biased against a section of mankind which has suffered untold agonies and atrocities in the past. He condemns Conrad's savage description which questions the very humanity of black people. He makes an assertion that as a sensible man, he will not accept any traveller's tales, not even a man's very eyes which he suspects them to be as jaundiced as Conrad's. He admits that Africans will have to strive hard to form a good image of Africa.

In his famous essay, 'Named for Victoria, Queen of England", Achebe talks about himself and his family. As a tribute to Victoria England, he got his name of Chinua Achebe, though earlier he was baptized as Albert Chinualumogu. In this essay, he talks about his father, who became the first Christian convert in his village. He compares his maternal uncle, who brought up his father, with Ezeulu of *Arrow of God* who did not raise any objection on his father joining the missionaries. He, like Ezeulu, thought that there was not any harm as it was a modern diversion. When Chinua's father got married, his maternal uncle was rather pleased with the white missionaries—both men and women, who came to attend the wedding in their fineries bearing gifts. Chinua asserts that though he was a thorough Christian, who sang hymns and read Bible night and day, he was fascinated by the ritual and the life of Igbos. He also talks about his life at the university where he got influenced by various books. When he read some appalling novels about Africa [including Joyce Cary's much praised *Mister Johnson*], he decided to tell about his own country to others. The realization had dawned upon him to remove the misconception about Africa from the minds of the people.

In his essay, "The Novelist as Teacher", he expresses his views on the kind of writing which the writers should do. He feels that the main job of a writer should be to educate the society, and not to worry much about what the readers wanted to read. Achebe does not seem anxious about the pattern of sales of his books in a year, which was about 800 copies in Britian; 20,000 in Nigeria; and about 2.500 in all other places. He expresses his contentment over his readers who enjoy reading his books and take that as an advice to them. Thus he seems to be quite satisfied with his role as a teacher in society.

His essay, "The Igbo world and its Art," talks about a multitude of forces which give Igbo life its restless dynamism. He feels that art has an outward, social and kinetic quality, where there is no room for contemplative privacy, as it enters into the public domain. He quotes examples of various art forms like traditional *mbari* figures and masquerades to show that the Igbos believe in transmitting the art to the whole community.

Achebe's another book of essays, *Home and Exile* (2000), is the great Nigerian Novelist's first book in more than ten years. It is a moving account of an exceptional life which captures the sense of threat and loss that the Africans experienced when their empire was invaded. Achebe also gives an account of his own intellectual life. In three elegant essays "My Home under Imperial Fire", "The Empire Fights Back" and "Today the Balance of Stories", he seeks to rescue culture from narratives written by Europeans. He describes about his homecoming to the town of Ogidi where his father had lived in the past. He remembers his childhood, the days which he spent in this town with his family. He talks about his parents who were uncompromising in their Christian beliefs, but had love for Igbo history and culture. He recalls his experience as a student in English schools in Nigeria. He talks about his first encounter with European perspectives on Africa in the works of Joyce Cary and Elspeth Huxley. He asserts that Joseph Conrad's description about Africans in his book *Heart of Darkness*, is evident of the fact that he did not consider Africans as humans like himself.

Achebe examines the controversial impact that his novel *Things Fall Apart* as well as his fellow Nigerian Amos Tutuola's *The Palm-Wine Drinkard* created on the readers. He even confronts the views of V.S. Naipaul about the colonial Africa. Achebe feels that Africa needs stories told by Africans and not by the outsiders. He feels that Africa is no longer the "great unknown" waiting to be discovered. The Empire is gone and the British population in Africa as well. He asserts that now the readers would like to know about Africa from the African writers—whether its Amos Tutuola, Wole Soyinka, or he himself. He reveals his heart before the readers, and expresses openly about his family and his country. He does not try to suppress the forces which work against the growth of Nigeria. He expects every writer to be a teacher who can guide the masses, and help reform the society. His optimism is quite prominent in his novels which attempts to form a new social order.

Today the whole nation feels that Achebe's influence should go on and on, teaching and reminding that all humankind is one. His characters, despite immense difficulties, fight to attain self-esteem for their society. No doubt, they could not achieve everything which they desired for, but proved themselves as better leaders. In an Interview with Chris Searle, Achebe said, "Okonkwo in *Things Fall Apart* or Ezeulu in *Arrow of God* did not fail. We are still talking about them. It is the same with the great leaders" (*Writing Across Worlds* 66).

Works Cited

Achebe, Chinua. *A Man of the People*. New York: Anchor, 1966.

______________ *Arrow of God*. New York: Anchor, 1974.

______________ *Girls at War and Other Stories*. New York: Anchor, 1973.

______________ *No Longer at Ease*. New York: Anchor, 1960.

______________ *The Trouble with Nigeria*. London: Heinemann, 1983.

______________ *Things Fall Apart*. New Delhi: Allied, 2004.

Barthold, Bonnie. J. *Black Time Fiction of Africa, The Caribbean and the United States*.New Haven: Conn:. Yale Univ. Press, 1981.

Singh, Thingnam Kishan. *Rethinking Colonialism: A Critique of the novels of* Chinua *Achebe and Ngu~gi~ wa Thiong'o*. Delhi: Worldview, 2006.

The Faber Book of Modern Verse. Journey of the Magi. Ed. Michael Roberts. Rev. Donald Hall. 3rd ed. London: Faber and Faber Limited, 1965.

"The Second Coming." London: Faber and Faber Limited, 1965.

Writing Across Worlds: Contemporary Writers talk. Ed. Susheila Nasta. London: Routledge, 2004.

6 Facts and Fantasy

The success of Achebe's novels, undoubtedly, lies in the beauty of his language. His novels bring a whole range of human experience before our mind's eye by use of imagery, drawn from both native and alien sources. His use of devices like proverbs, myths, and legends enriches the English language and speaks of the rich Igbo culture. His language is not merely a technique, but an embodiment of African civilization. His novels teach and instruct through prayers, speeches, and song sequences. They are not just entertainment, but they direct the lives of the readers. It was the rituals, language, myths, and legends of the Igbo society which bound the people together. The relationship between a husband and a wife, a son and a father, and a mother and a daughter, got cemented though various rituals which they performed and the legends which they narrated to each other. Though the whole world called them 'primitive' and 'backward', they were happy and contented in their own world. Chinua Achebe captures the 'anarchy' brought about by Colonialism and Christianity in Ibo society. The rituals and customs became a symbol of lawlessness due to the arrival of Europeans. The *Weekly Star* of 15 May 1983 has this on its front page under the title, 'The Nigerian and Corruption': "Keeping an average Nigerian from being corrupt is like keeping a goat from eating yam" (Achebe, *The Trouble with Nigeria* 38).

In the traditional Igbo society, the offering of the 'Kola nut' signified politeness and warmth towards a visitor. But in post colonial society, Chinua presents 'Kola nut' as the only 'palm-fruit' of the village which signified corruption. In his novels, visitors were offered a Kola nut, some alligator pepper, and a lump of white chalk. The Ibo people used to draw some lines on the floor with the chalk and then painted their toe. When the Kola nut was broken by the visitor, the people sitting over prayed to their ancestors for life and health, and for protection against their enemies. The main protagonist of *Things Fall Apart* Okonkwo, when offered the Kola nut to the guests said: "I have brought you this little Kola. As our people say, a man who pays respect to the great paves the way for his own greatness" (Achebe 18). The ritual of kola nut which taught the Ibo people tolerance and respect for each other, lost its significance in due course of time. Achebe does not feel hesitant to show the impact of colonialism on the rituals of Ibo society which made the people corrupt outside the traditional society. The 'Kola nut' which symbolized warmth in Igbo society, was now in modern society equal to the offering of 'bribe'. In *No Longer at Ease,* Obi Okonkwo is offered bribe by Mr. Mark to get a Federal scholarship to study in England. His mind is not at peace for the reason that he refused to accept the bribe. He feels like an inexperienced kite that carried away a duckling, and was ordered by its mother to return it because the duck had said nothing, made no noise, just walked away. Obi could realize his inability to cope up with the prevalent system which makes him corrupt. Achebe expresses the Igbo mentality that, "a man

Figure 18. Life of Igbo people

Source: Electronic.

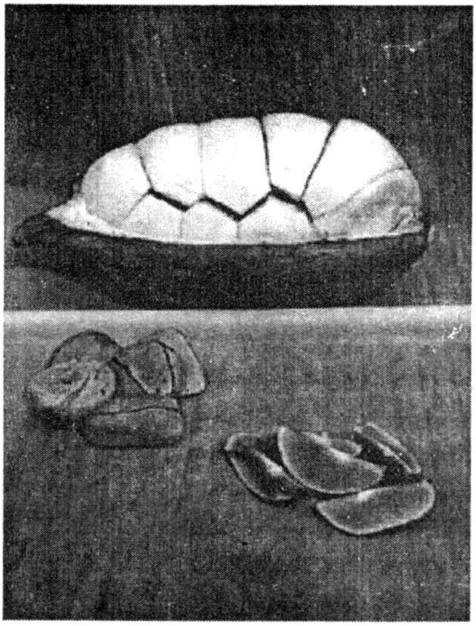

Fig 19. Kola nut

Source: Electronic.

expects you to accept "Kola" from him for services rendered, and until you do, his mind is never at rest"(Achebe, *No Longer at Ease* 100). He also shows the tolerance of the people for the corrupt practices. He realises the accepted fact of the society that, "...the trouble was not in receiving bribes, but in failing to do the thing for which the bribe was given?" (Achebe 100-101).

Corruption became a ritual in Igbo society. In "The Voter" in *Girls at War,* the people of Umuofia expected bribe from the political parties in order to support their candidature. So when Ezenwa and other elders receive two shillings from Roof and his assistant on behalf of Marcus, the leader of the People's Alliance Party, Ezenwa expresses his dissatisfaction over the meagre amount:

> We shall, every one of us, drop his paper for Marcus. Who would leave an *ozo* feast and go to a poor ritual meal ? Tell Marcus he has our papers, and our wives' papers too. But what we do say is that two shillings is shameful (Achebe 16).

Achebe, in his short story collection, *Girls at War,* also writes about the other party, P.A.P. [Progressive Organization Party], which was even ready to give out pounds, not shillings, as they knew that the people of Umuofia would listen and vote for them. In *The Trouble with Nigeria,* Achebe admits that the Nigerians became corrupt due to the influence of colonialism and Western education. He blames the political and economic system for this. He realizes the need for strict and stringent laws so that a man does not get a chance to accept the bribe. He supports a system which does not make corruption easy and profitable, but makes it difficult and inconvenient.

In Achebe's novels, names of some of the characters show that the Igbos gave much importance to the 'naming ceremony'. In Igbo week, as there are four days, they name the Igbo as Okonkwo—born on the *nkwo* day, i.e., the first day of the week. Those born on the second, third, and fourth day of the week were named as Okeke, Okoye, or Okafo. In Chinua's novels, all these names find place signifying their love for traditional Igbo names. The Igbos strongly believe in reincarnation as they feel it to be one of the ways to share their love with their loved ones who have passed. They believe that death by suicide was a 'bad death' which did not allow one to reincarnate. In *Things Fall Apart,* when Okonkwo commits suicide, it is taken as one of the most horrendous of all offences against the earth goddess. His clansmen neither touched his corpse nor buried him with all the rites due to a great warrior and an *ozo,* as they did when Ogbuefi Ezeudu died. Rather the elders had to offer sacrifices to cleanse the desecrated ground which Okonkwo had polluted.

Achebe, in his novels, has reflected the Igbos' cosmology, where there is *Chukwu* or *ama ama amasi amasi* [the one who can never be fully understood]. Below him are shown a number of deities whose domains may be limited to specific aspects of life on earth. There are no private collections among the Igbo beyond personal ritual objects like the ikenga—a carved piece of wood whom they worshipped as God. There is a mentioning of Amadiora—the god of the thunder, Ufiojioku—the god of the harvest, and Anyanwu—the sungod. Principal among these deities is Ani-the Earth goddess, who is the arbiter of ethical conduct. Achebe has shown the life of the Igbos which was guided by the ethics of the community. In case they transgressed any of the rules, they were expected to atone for their offences by performing prescribed ritual acts of expiation. In *Things Fall Apart*, Achebe has shown the existence of evil spirits—*umunadi*, who were believed to live in the uninhabited spaces beyond the village settlements and also in the bad bush. He admits the existence of *ogbanje*—the spirits of children, who reincarnate and are born to die, often in infancy, only to be born again by the same or another unfortunate mother. He also throws light on the Igbo thought that there can be no impaired manifestation of any force or being, and that human agency is essential to the realization of one's destiny.

Fig 20. Ritual object, *Ikenga*

Source: Electronic.

Though Achebe's love and concern for Ibo society is prominent, he clearly reflects the backwardness of the society by throwing light on the status of women. While the men used to go out for hunting with loaded guns, women took care of the household. Achebe's perception of woman's status seems to resemble the thoughts of the Victorian Poet—Alfred Tennyson, who related men to field and women to hearth. Palm-wine was offered to the women by their husbands in the order of their seniority. They had to go down on one knee, drink a little from the horn, and hand over the same to their husbands. In *Things Fall Apart,* Anasi, being the first wife of Okonkwo, was the first to receive a horn of wine from her husband. And then the other wives could drink in the same fashion by kneeling down on one leg. Achebe seems to show that it was a custom to maintain the dependency of Igbo women on men. The women considered their husbands as idols who made them bent in front of them to get crushed later.

Achebe signifies the importance of the New Yam Festival, which was celebrated by Igbos every year before the harvest began, to honour the earth goddess and the ancestral spirits of the clan. Achebe exhibits the excitement among the Igbos on the New Yam Festival and on other important occasions. In his novels, there is a mentioning of wood, clay, and metal instruments used by the musicians who were all gay, and sang the latest song in the village. He feels that the ceremony which is called Mbari among the Igbo people, is a festival of art, a celebration of humanity. He is of the opinion that it is not a festival of oral arts; it is more a festival of the visual arts, the plastic arts, though drama and songs are presented there as well. At the time of feasts, pots of yam pottage, *foofoo,* bitter-leaf soup and *egusi* soup, boiled legs of goat, large bowls of cooked asa fish, and kegs of sweet wine tapped from the raffia palm were enjoyed by the Igbos. Achebe depicts warmth and love in the Igbo society which believed that a person who treated his brother worse than a stranger could be called as a fool.

Traditionally, the Igbos, especially Igbo women, believed in decorating their bodies for a variety of reasons including aesthetics. The Igbos believe in the saying that one's body is one's temple. On the festival of pumpkin leaves, Achebe talks of the Igbo women who wore their finest clothes and ornaments of ivory and jigida or waist beads according to the wealth of their husbands.

On special occasions, they used to paint themselves with cam wood and drew black patterns of uli and faint yellow lines of ogalu on their body. In *Things Fall Apart* (TFA), when a suitor visited Akueke, she wore a coiffure which was done up into a crest in the middle of the head. Cam wood was rubbed lightly into her skin, and all over her body were black patterns drawn with uli.

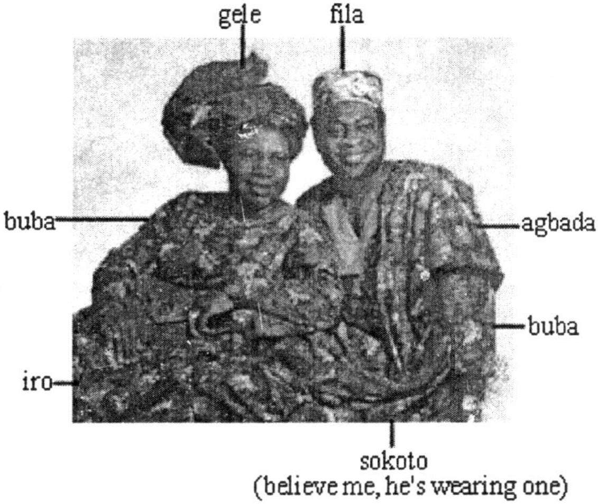

Fig 21. Costume of Igbo people

Source: Electronic.

On her arms were red and yellow bangles, and on her waist four or five rows of *jigida*, or waist-beads. Igbo men wore loincloth underneath and a thick coarse toga over it. In *Arrow of God*, Ezeulu held on his right hand a long, iron, walking-staff with a sharp, spear-like lower end which every titled man carried on special occasions. At this point in history, the only purpose of clothing in Igboland was to cover private parts. Children are believed to have nothing to hide and so usually were naked. A child may wear a string of beads around the waist for medicinal purposes or reasons. Igbo women always carried babies on their backs with a strip of clothing. In most cases, women did not have to cover the breast area, as it can be seen in Achebe's novel *Things Fall Apart*: "Ekwefi began to run, holding her breasts with her hands to stop them flapping noisily against her body" (93). Additionally, men were loin clothes to cover their private parts. The loin clothes would go under the crotch and were tied together with a rope around the waist. This type of clothing gave men the required freedom for performing various jobs like farming, hunting, palm wine tapping, and wrestling. The titled men—*ozo*, wore special treads on their ankles. Achebe mentions several times in TFA that men carried goatskin bags in which they kept essential items such as their drinking horns—animal's horns—as well as snuff-bottle, and its spoon. In this novel, Okonkwo drank palm-wine from his first human head [his first war victim] on great occasions such as the funeral of a village celebrity.

Achebe reflects the customs and traditions which bound the Ibo people together in the precolonial society. But with the changing course of time, their faith could not remain intact. In TFA, during the 'Week of Peace', when a man was not suppose to say a harsh word to his neighbours, Okonkwo beat his wife badly for which he was punished, as was the custom, by Ezeani—the Priest of the earth goddess. This custom of Igbos reminds the Indians of the belief of the Jains which forbids them to be harsh for fifteen days during the celebration of *Paryushan*.

In *Arrow of God*, the ritual of disposing off the yams of the old year, is used as a weapon by the white man to develop Igbos faith in the new religion and new culture. When Ezeulu could not call for 'New Yam Festival' as the time had not come for it, for the reason that three yams were left instead of one from the last, a new member of Good country's church committee said: "So we can tell our heathen brethren to bring their one yam to church instead of giving it to Ulu ?" (Achebe 215). Achebe shows how the ritual of New Yam Festival led to the conversion of the Igbos to Christianity, thereby deteriorating their own customs and traditions. And one who joined the church ceased to be "people of nothing" and were called the "people of the church" (Achebe, *No Longer at Ease* 66). He also shows the increasing importance of the High God in 'traditional' religion, and the tendency to identify Chukwu [in Igboland] with the Christian God. Christianity set children apart from all other Ibo children as they were not allowed to accept food in their neighbour's house if they offered their food to idols. Though Achebe himself was a thorough Christian, the idols and the food offered to them, had a strange pull on him. Achebe in *Hopes and Impediments* says that,"what I do remember is a fascination for the ritual and the life on the other arm of the crossroad" (35).

In *No Longer at Ease,* Chinua highlights the influence of western education on Obi Okonkwo. He was sent to England so that he could serve his society later. Umuofia—an Ibo village in

Eastern Nigeria, had made the sacrifice for getting him a scholarship to study abroad. But for the sake of an *osu*—an outcaste girl, he becomes willing to stand against his society. He is unable to understand the traditional customs in the modern era:

> It was scandalous that in the middle of the twentieth century a man could be barred from marrying a girl simply because her great-great-great-great grandfather had been dedicated to serve a god, thereby setting himself apart and turning his descendants into a forbidden caste to the end of Time. Quite unbelievable (82).

In closely-knit African Society, the importance of language is seen in pristine clarity. The Igbos used Igbo or Kwa language which produced magical impact on the minds of the people. Writing about Igbo society in Nigeria, Igwe and Green had this to say:

> A speaker who could use language effectively and had a good command of idioms and proverbs was respected by his fellows and was often a leader in the community (qtd. in Achebe, *Hopes and Impediments* 130).

Achebe has used Pidgin English in his texts, a language which reflects the way English is actually used by some Nigerians. It is liberally sprinkled with Ibo vocabulary, so that it gives a feel of the native speech. In *The Empire Writes Back,* Bill Ashcroft, Gareth Griffiths, and Helen Tiffin describe about the linguistic reality of pidgin as it functioned in colonial times:

> Pidgin was inevitably used in the context of master- servant relationships during the period of European Colonization.... Of course, pidgin remains a dominant mode of discourse among all non-English-speakers wherever it exists, but its role in most literature..., is both to install class difference and to signify its presence (75).

In *A Man of the People,* Chinua writes about the Chief Nanga who always spoke English or pidgin, and Mrs. Nanga who stuck to Igbo language with the odd English words 'thrown in now and again', "Hallo, hawa you. Nice to see you again. All na lie lie"(36). In *Anthills of Savannah,* Achebe writes in cockney, a variety of pidgin English. He uses it especially when he portrays the woman as being stupid, but then she talks about Shakespeare, "Your boys like us, ain' they? My girlfriend saiz it's the Desdemona complex. Nice word Desde-mona. Italian I think. Ever hear it?" (73-74).

Being born at the crossroads of cultures, Chinua Achebe accepts the influence of colonialism on the Igbo language. He expresses himself by saying that he has always been fond of Igbo language which was spoken with eloquence by the old men of the village. He loved the stories narrated to him in his native language. He states that he learnt English at the age of eight. He feels that this language became so dominant that probably he has spoken more words in English than Igbo. Achebe's love for Igbo language is quite clear by the way he uses African proverbs, imagery, and metaphors in his novels. In 1964, Achebe in a speech entitled, "The African writer and the English Language", said:

> Is it right that a man should abandon his mother tongue for someone else's? It looks like a dreadful betrayal and produces a guilty feeling. But for me there is no other choice. I have been given the language and I intend to use it (qtd. in Thiong'o, *Decolonising the Mind* 7).

According to Achebe, 'Igbo' exists in numerous dialects which vary from village to village, but there is no standardized formal written or oral language that all Igbo use in Western Africa. No doubt, Christian missionanies tried to create and impose one – 'Union Igbo' – in order to translate the *Bible* and speed up the religious conversion in the late nineteenth century. Unlike Ngũgĩ wa Thiong'o, who worked for the abolition of the English department as a step towards cultural decolonization, Achebe does not comment on the abandonment of European languages. He feels that sixty languages of his country cannot be officially used thereby disintegrating his state into sixty states. So Achebe feels that:

> ...An African and a nationalist looking at the situation now, there is a real value in keeping our countries together using a language that has been imposed upon us (*Writing Across Worlds* 68).

Ngũgĩ wa Thiong'o feels that to come into contact with English, is to come into contact with something both negative and positive, and the positive has as much as any product of any other language. But he asserts that the novels written by African writers like Chinua Achebe and few others, reflect a world—a colonial world, and this world is really their world. He asserts that the African countries, as colonies and even today as neo-colonies, define themselves in terms of the languages of Europe. They are called English–speaking, French–speaking, or Portuguese-speaking African countries.

In African literature—stories, dramas, riddles, histories, myths, songs, proverbs, and other expressions—are frequently employed to educate and entertain children. Oral histories, myths, and proverbs additionally serve to remind the whole community of their ancestor's heroic deeds, their past, and the precedents of their customs and traditions. The archetypes and symbols used by Wole Soyinka in his works are drawn from the myths of different cultures—Classical, Judaeo-Christian, Yoruba, and even Indian. About this Wole Soyinka in his interview with Mary David says:

> I think it means very obviously that humanity has – civilizations have — a lot more in common than they profess, than they are willing to accept (Soyinka, *Writing Across Worlds* 23).

Achebe's characters pepper their speech with proverbs: "Among the Ibo the art of conversation is regarded very highly, and proverbs are the palm-oil with which words are eaten" (Achebe, TFA 6). The sensibility and wisdom of the Igbo people becomes visible in the usage of proverbs which reflects the characters' behaviour and manner. Ngũgĩ wa Thiong'o feels that Achebe's *Things Fall Apart* and *Arrow of God* (AOG), Amos Tutuola's *The Palmwine Drinkard,* and Gabriel Okara's *The Voice* could use the borrowed tongues in the best way, by making them 'prey' on African proverbs, and other peculiarities of African speech and folklore. But to show the powerlessness of Igbos due to colonial rule, Achebe has deliberately avoided the use of proverbs in the third and final part of TFA. He makes prolific use of proverbs which reflect the good and the lean times which their societies experienced. He uses a number of proverbs which shows Ibo's belief about spirituality. In his novel *Things Fall Apart,* Okonkwo said 'yes' very strongly for all the responsibilities laid on him by his society, as he knew that,"When a man says yes his *chi* [Personal God], says yes also" (25). Achebe seems to relate *'chi'* to the inner conscience, thereby stressing on the thought that 'God resides in oneself'. If one feels that one can do it, he can make his life a heaven, and if one is negative about oneself, then he can make his life a hell. Other proverbs used in Achebe's novels such as "mother is supreme" (TFA 121), communicate Ibo views on society. It shows their belief that when a man falls into misfortune, as in the case of Okonkwo of *Things Fall Apart*, he seeks solace at his mother's place.

Many of Achebe's proverbs concern matters of power and politics, particularly related to the impact of colonization. In *Arrow of God*, when Ezeulu, the Chief Priest of Ulu, anticipates of something wrong by the white, he addresses the assembled rulers of Umuaro. He firstly thanks them as the belief of Igbos is that,"If you thank a man for what he has done he will have strength to do more" (Achebe 142). And when Ezeulu goes to the white man's prison, people's indifferent attitude towards him has been cited in the proverbs like, "the lizard who threw confusion into his mother's funeral rite, did he expect outsiders to carry the burden of honouring his dead (125). For their arrogance, Ezeulu and Okonkwo can be compared to, "the little bird *nza* who so far forgot himself after a heavy meal that he challenged his *chi*"(TFA 28, AOG 14). Even in the mythologies of many cultures, the little bird *nza* resembles some of the characters who also challenged the gods. They include the Sumerian hero—Gilgamesh, and Greek characters such as Prometheus, Sisyphus, and Tantalus.

A body of myths or sacred tales used by the Igbos to explain their problems and mysteries of life and death find a prominent place in Achebe's novels. He feels that the folk tales which the ancestors crafted, must be communicated to the next generations showing its value, importance, and significance:

> Because they [our forefathers and ancestors] are so far away and because we are surrounded by the tumult and distractions of daily life they have to shout and repeat themselves not only in phrase after phrase but also in myth after myth, varying the form slightly now and again until the central message goes home (*Hopes and Impediments* 136).

In *Things Fall Apart*, Achebe shows various aspects of the traditional belief system that may be dismissed as superstitious, as having an internal logic. The recurrent cycle of death and rebirth [ogbanje], which torments Ekwefi's child Ezinma, is summarily arrested when a diviner digs up the item *iyi-uwa*—a pebble binding her to the cycle. It was the belief of the igbos that if the child was an *ogbanje*—a wicked child, then he entered his mother's wombs to be born again. So few years back for Ezinma's survival, a medicine-man had dug up earth to hide Ezinma's *iyi-uwa,* the pebble in a rag.

The myths provided the Igbos a counter to the dispossession due to changing times, and a stay against times acceleration. Achebe has quoted many myths of the Igbo people in Nigeria which bear more directly on the question of language. One myth related to life shows the man's desire for immortality which does not become possible:

> When death first entered the world, men sent a messenger to Chuku, asking him whether the dead could not be restored to life and sent back to their old homes. They chose the dog as their messenger.
>
> The dog, however, did not go straight to Chuku, and dallied on the way.The toad had overheard the message, and as he wished to punish mankind, he overtook the dog and reached Chuku first. He said he had been sent by men to say that after death they had no desire at all to return to the world. Chuku declared that he would respect their wishes, and when the dog arrived with the true message he refused to alter his decision.
>
> Thus although a human being may be born again, he cannot return with the same body and the same personality (qtd. in *Hopes and Impediments,* 136).

In *Things Fall Apart* and *Arrow of God,* the women narrated the folk tales to the children at night which they always enjoyed. The folktale tellers used call-response techniques. And a *griot* [praise singer] used to accompany the narrative with a music to renew the attentiveness of the audience by drawing their participation into the lyric performance:

> Tell the mother her child is crying
> Tell the mother her child is crying
> And then prepare a stew of uziza
> And also a stew of uziza...
> (*Arrow of God* 186).

In *Things Fall Apart*, Ekwefi, Okonkwo's wife narrates a traditional Igbo folktale to her daughter, Ezinma which dramatizes a moral. It relates to a cunning tortoise [Nnabe] who manages to befool the birds [Chineke] at the feast and enjoys the food all alone. But at the end, he is punished for his selfishness, and he falls from the sky thereby breaking his shell into pieces. Achebe explains that the trickster tortoise is a favourite in Igbo children's stories, for he "is a character that children can be related to. He is rogue, but he is nice kind of rogue" ("African Storytelling"). The tortoise has been depicted as a trickster figure in African folklore. Achebe, in his interview with Jerome Brooks, Admits that he himself loved stories, stories told in their home, firstly by his mother, then by his elder sister, especially the story of the tortoise [called Nnabe in Igbo cultures, Ijapa in Yoruban cultures, and Fudugazi in Zulu culture].

The folktales mentioned by Achebe in his novels make an attempt to reform the society, thereby getting rid of one's weaknesses. Ikemefuna's song in *Things Fall Apart* is a condensed version of an Igbo folktale which warns the king to not to commit an action that would indulge with his high office and prosperity of people. Like the king in Ikemefuna's song, Okonkwo is warned against committing a sin by killing a child whom he sheltered for three years and called him his father:

> Eze elina, elina !
> Sala
> Eze ilikwa ya
> Ikwaba akwa oligholi
> Ebe Danda nechi eze
> Ebe Uzuzu nete egwu
> Sala (Achebe 54).

Emmanuel Obiechina offered a line-by- line English translation of the Igbo folktale:

> [the singer calls:]
> King, do not eat [it], do not eat !

Sala [the audience responds]

> King, if you eat it
> You will weep for the abomination
> Where Danda [white ant] installs king

Where Uzuzu [Dust] dances to the drums
Sala [the audience responds] ("African Story telling").

In short story, "Chike's School Days", in *Girls at War*, Achebe uses the singing technique to portray the colonial impact on Africans. Chike in his village school, attended "religious class" where they sang and sometimes danced the catechism. They even sang songs in English. Chike often sang "Ten Green Bottles," especially the first and the last lines, the middle he hummed and mumbled:

Ten grin botr angin on dar war,
Ten grin botr angin on dar war,
Hm hm hm hm hm
Hm, hm hm hm hm hm,
An ten grin botr angin on dar war (41).

In *No Longer at Ease*, Achebe reflects the influence of the western culture on Nigerians by the songs sung on various occasions. At the ball, the Europeans held their women close, breast to breast, so that they could dance uninterrupted. When instead of Obi, Clara danced with Obi's friend Christopher, the vocalist sang this song on the microphone:

I was playing moi guitar jeje,
A Lady gave me a kiss.
Her husband didn't like it,
He had to drag him wife away.
Gentlemen, please hold your wife.
Father and mum, please hold your girls.
The calypso is so nice,
If they follow, don't blame Bobby (129).

In Achebe's novels, the Igbos love for nature becomes prominent in the songs sung by the children especially the rain songs. In *Anthills of the Savannah*, the children sung a childish rain song to express happiness: "Ogwogwo mmili takumei ayolo!" (87). In *A Man of the people*, when Odili waits at Chief Nanga's house in order to meet Edna, he gives out three Shillings to three different groups of boys and their masked dancers who danced comically to the song:

Sunday, bigi bele Sunday, bigi bele
Akatakata done come!
Everybody run away!
Sunday, Alleluia! (98).

Achebe's empathy with his ancestral culture is evident in the harmonies that he reveals between the people and their environment. Such harmonies are predicated on the music of drums, which conveys a sense of rhythm that defined the culture of the people over time. Amos Tutuola in his work, *The Palm-Wine Drinkard,* signifies the role of the three fellows—Drum, Song, and Dance. Such is the power of their music that:

> "People who had been dead for hundreds of years rose up and came to witness":
>
> The whole people of the new town, the whole people that rose up from the grave, animals, snakes, Spirits and other nameless creatures... (qtd.in Achebe, *Hopes and Impediments* 105-106).

Fig 22. Ancestral mask

Source: Electronic.

In Igbo society, the significance of the ancestral spirits known as 'egwugwu', who appeared in ancestral masks, cannot be undermined. Each egwugwu represented a village of the clan whose leader was called the 'Evil Forest'. Symbolizing the ancestors of the community, these elders arbitrated public disputes and their authority was never challenged by anyone. The drum was sounded and the flute was blown to mark the arrival of the spirits.

Chinua Achebe, in his novels, especially *Arrow of God,* shows the arrival of a new mask on the crest of excitement:

> The face held power and terror; each exposed tooth was the size of a big man's thumb, the eyes were large sockets as big as a fist, two gnarled horns pointed upwards and inwards above its head nearly touching at the tip. It carried a shield of skin in the left hand and a huge matchet in the right (198-199).

In *Writing Across Worlds,* in an interview with Mary David, Wole Soyinka appreciates the African mask as an aesthetic object. He talks about the elevation of the mask saying:

> ...I know how it is worn. I happen to know the rest of the mask that the carrier wears. I know what shapes he makes as he dances. At such times I am able to go deeper and contemplate its meaning because it is also a ritual form—incidentally, of renewal—and it is part and parcel of the ceremonies (24).

In *Arrow of God,* there is a mentioning of Udala trees in Umuaro which were sacred to ancestral spirits. The belief of the Africans here seems to resemble with that of the Indians during the Vedic period. Just as the Pipal tree was significant for Indians, the Udala tree was holy for the Nigerians. In Igbo society, if anyone tried to harm the trees, they had to pay heavy fines and sacrifices. The Chief Priest, Ezeulu, preserved the continuity of the cycle of spiritual-political power, through a monthly ritual sacrifice of white chick, grown cocks, yellowish palm fronds, and lobes of kolanut. In *Things Fall Apart,* after Okonkwo's suicide at the end of the novel, the village elders are about to offer sacrifices to cleanse the land.

Darkness held a vague terror for Ibo, even for the bravest of them.Children were warned not to whistle at night for the fear of evil spirits. They considered animals as more dangerous in the dark. A snake was never called by its name at night, because it would hear. Rather it was called a string. Even today Indians living in rural areas dread snakes at night and call it a 'dori', that is, a string. They even warn their children to not to blow whistle for fear of evil spirits. Just as in Indian society, king Cobra is worshipped and is considered sacred, Achebe reflects the Igbo society where killing a python was considered as an abomination. In *Things Fall Apart,* "Is that me?" was the way people answered calls from outside (38). They never answered 'yes' for the fear that it might be a sinister calling. In Chinua's novels, 'things really fall apart,' and the Igbos old mythology and religion did lose some of their hold. In *Things Fall Apart,* the egwugwu—the ancestral spirits were exposed to public gaze by overzealous converts, and Okoli dies not long after he kills a sacred python. But the new mission—the Christian mission thrives, within the dreaded Evil Forest, with a growing number of converts.

Works Cited

Achebe, Chinua. *A Man of the People*. New York : Anchor, 1966.

______________ *Anthills of the Savannah*. New York : Anchor, 1987.

______________ *Arrow of God*. New York : Anchor, 1974.

______________ *Girls at War and Other Stories*. New York: Anchor, 1973.

______________ *Hopes and Impediments : Selected Essays*. New York: Anchor, 1988.

______________ *No Longer at Ease*. New York : Anchor, 1960.

______________ *The Trouble with Nigeria*. London : Heinemann, 1983.

______________ *Things Fall Apart*. New Delhi : Allied, 2004.

Agatucci, Cora. "African Storytelling." *Article*. 2005 *http://web.cocc.edu/cagatucci/classes/hum211/afrstory* htm.

Ashcroft, Bill, Griffiths Gareth, and Tiffin Helen. *The Empire Writes Back*. 2nd ed. London : Routledge, 2002.

Ngũgĩ wa Thiong'o, *Decolonising the Mind : The Politics of Language in African Literature*. Delhi : Worldview, 1986.

Writing Across Worlds: Contemporary Writers talk. Ed. Susheila Nasta. London : Routledge, 2004.

7 Exploration of the Voiceless Female Characters

Achebe's female characters are silent, voiceless and invisible, whose status is no more than a household object. In his novels, he has depicted the Ibo society where anything strong is likened to man, and anything weak to woman. The women of the household were ruled with a heavy hand, and the wives were not allowed to question their husbands about their decisions. Achebe who is criticized as a sexist author, doesnot show much change in the state of woman's condition in the precolonial and postcolonial time-period. Even Rose Ure Mezu in his article expresses that:

> ...Nigeria's traditional culture, Muslim as well as non-Muslim, had been masculine-based even before the advent of the white man...Colonial rule merely aggravated the situation by introducing a lopsided system in which African men received a well-rounded education while..., African women received only utilitarian, cosmetic skills in Domestic Science Centers... ("Women in Achebe's World").

In *Uncle Tom's Cabin,* Harriet Beecher Stowe has given a pathetic state of slave trade of African girls. Achebe highlights the low status of women in Ibo society, whereas Stowe hits on the slave trade which exploited the voiceless female characters. The slave mother knew that she could be at the whim of her common owner and be separated from her children:

> The fellow that was trading for her didn't want her baby...She squeezed up her child in her arms, and talked, and went on real awful...when they carried off the child, and locked her up, She jest went ravin' mad, and died in a week (7).

Fig 23. An African woman.

Source: Electronic.

Achebe has depicted the Ibo society where men were allowed to marry many times depending on their economic status. It resembles the Islamic culture which also permits a man to marry four times as per his economic status. Though in the past, these marriages were conditional, today in the modern age, this practice is being misused by men. In *Things Fall Apart*, Achebe has presented an androcentric world where the man is everything and the woman nothing. As Leonard A. Podis and Saaka Yakubu note that, "The African male may be seen to occupy simultaneously the role of oppressed (in relation to the colonial masters) and oppressor (in relation to the African Women)" ("Watermarks"). Children were considered to be an asset for the family. A wealthy man was one who possessed more number of wives and children. Nwakibee was called a rich man as he had three huge barns, nine wives and 30 children. Yam, the king of crops, was a man's crop whereas coco-yams, beans, and cassava were the woman's crops. According to Nigerian critic Juliet Okonkwo:

> Achebe's cultural universe is one in which women [are] to be seen not heard, coming and going, with mounds of foofoo, pots of water, market baskets, fetching Kola, being scolded and beaten before they disappear behind the huts of their compound ("Women in Achebe's World").

In *Things Fall Apart*, during the Week of Peace, Okonkwo beat his youngest wife, Ojiugo as she was not at home and had gone to plait her hair at her friend's house. Achebe seems to show that women were not trusted in society for the reason that, 'to be a virgin' was quite unusual, rather a distinct thing. Okonkwo also gave Ekwefi, his second wife, a sound beating who had merely cut a few leaves off to wrap some food. He even chased her with a loaded gun when she murmured something about the guns that never shot. In Igbo society, the desire for woman was like a desire to conquer and subdue. In *Things Fall Apart*, Okonkwo never showed any emotion openly, unless it be the emotion of anger. In order to exhibit his strength, he shouted at his daughter Ezinma, "Sit like a woman !"(Achebe 40). And she had no other choice than to bring her two legs together and stretch in front of her.

Achebe exhibits Igbo as patriarchal societies, which treasured their sons more highly than their daughters. The boys' duty ranged from washing their father's clothing, taking care of the flock, getting the yam seedling reeds, getting the knives, and other farming implements ready for farm work. They also got involved in masquerades, wrestling matches, meetings, and even accompanied their father to ceremonies. But a girls' world began and ended with getting married, getting children, and serving the meal needs of their husband with the kitchen as the headquarters of their functions. Even in Indian society, this feature is quite prominent where the boys are more privileged than the girls. In *Of Woman Born* (1977), Adrienne Rich unwittingly captures all the nuances of the African traditional social milieu when she describes patriarchy as:

> The power of the fathers: a familial, social, ideological, and political system in which, by direct pressure—or through tradition, law and language, customs, etiquette, education, and division of labor—men determine what parts women shall or shall not play, and the female is everywhere subsumed by the male ("Women in Achebe's World").

In *Things Fall Apart* (TFA), the society's concern for the survival of the lineage is expressed in such names as Amaechina [may the compound not perish / disappear], or Obiechina [may the household not perish]. As these families expected more from boys than girls, they exerted greater pressure on the boys to succeed than on the girls. Okonkwo, the central character in Achebe's novel TFA, tells his boys stories about violence, tribal wars, and blood sheds to prepare them for their future role as guardians, defenders, and the masters of their family. He wants his son Nwoye to grow into a tough young man capable of ruling his father's household by controlling his womenfolk: "I will not have a son who cannot hold up his head in the gathering of the clan. I would sooner strangle him with my own hands" (30).

On the contrary, Achebe has shown the girls as very soft, weak, and tender. Mothers told their daughters various stories so as to teach them how to behave to attract their husbands and win their hearts. In TFA, Nwoye gets interested more in tales of animals than in his father's stories:

> Nwoye...somehow he still preferred the stories that his mother used to tell... stories of the tortoise and his wily ways.... But he now knew that they were for foolish women and children, and he knew that his father wanted him to be a man. And so he feigned that he no longer cared for women's stories. And when he did this he saw that his father was pleased, and no longer rebuked him or beat him (Achebe 48-49).

The irony in TFA is that Okonkwo's boy Nwoye runs away from his father, while his sister Ezinma, dotes on Okonkwo. It was not only that this surprising bond was there in between the father and his daughter, Okonkwo even wishes if Ezinma were a boy:

> "You have not eaten for two days," said his daughter Ezinma when she brought the food to him. "So you must finish this."

> She sat down and stretched her legs in front of her. Okonkwo ate the food absent-mindedly. 'She should have been a boy', he thought as he looked at his ten-year-old daughter (57-58).

Achebe also shows another incidence to emphasize on the bond between Okonkwo and Ezinwa. While on exile, when Okonkwo expresses his desire that she should hold off getting married until his return to Umuofia, Ezinma dismisses all good suitors from Mbanta, their place of exile.

In his novel, *Things Fall Apart,* Achebe depicts Okonkwo as a self-decisive man who didnot like women of the household to question him. When Okonkwo brought Ikemefuna home, he was questioned by Anasi, his seniormost wife about his duration of stay. Okonkwo replied that: "Do what you are told, woman. When did you become one of the *ndichie* of Umuofia?" (14). In *Arrow of God,* Ezeulu didnot allow his wives to open their mouth in front of him, and to question his decision. When he chose Oduche, one of his sons to join the white man, he told Ugoye, his wife that: "How does it concern you what I do with my sons ?"(Achebe 46). Ezeulu was even rude to his wife Matefi and warned her by saying: "If you want that madness of yours to be cured, bring my supper at this time another day..."(9). Achebe shows that the women were not engaged in any of the discussions, or the councils of war. They didnot form part of the masquerades representing the judiciary and ancestral spirits. It reminds one of the Zamindari system prevalent in India, especially in U.P, Bihar, and Rajasthan in the nineteenth century when the women were suppressed by men. They didnot have any say in the decisionmaking of the household, rather were considered as outsiders.

'Weakness' symbolized 'women' in Igbo society. In Achebe's novel, *Things Fall Apart,* when Ikemefuna, fourteen year boy whom Okonkwo loved for three years appeals to him to not to kill him, he is 'dazed' with fear of his becoming womanly. His furious manhood empowers everything feminine in his life, including his own conscience. This was because they reminded him of his father's laziness and cowardice. After killing Ikemefuna, Okonkwo, who could not understand why he was so distraught, asks himself: "When did you become a shivering old woman..."(59). And when the elders of Mbanta refused to wage war against the Christians because they thought that it was not their custom to fight for their gods, Okonkwo's reaction is characteristic:

> "Let us not reason like cowards," said Okonkwo. "If a man comes into my hut and defaecates on the floor, what do I do? Do I shut my eyes? No! I take a stick and break his head. That is what a man does. These people are daily pouring filth over us, and Okeke says we should pretend not to see." Okonkwo made a sound full of disgust. This was a womanly clan, he thought (TFA 145).

In his reflection of the Ibo society, Achebe gives emphasis on a woman's capacity to give birth to more children and especially to sons. In *Things Fall Apart,* the husbands used to slaughter a goat for their wives if she bore third son in succession. Ayi Kwei Armah also asserts with the Achebe's description of the African female characters. Like Achebe, Armah also shows the female figures suffering because of the colonization of their houses, conquered by their husbands. Women only seem to be wives, enslaved by a chain of many unwanted pregnancies. Some gatherings in TFA were specially for men on which Achebe comments:

> It was clear from the way the crowd stood or sat that the ceremony was for men. There were many women, but they looked on from the fringe like outsiders (79).

Achebe presents the Igbo culture as patriarchal, where the women have been depicted as "outsiders," looking on from the "fringe," and not participating in the administration of justice. Achebe's women pray to Igbo gods for an end to European dominion because the ancient Igbo tradition appears to them as the only one 'land' that Britain is not allowed to conquer.

In Achebe's novel *Things Fall Apart,* Anasi being the first wife of Okonkwo, looked every inch the ruler of the womenfolk, in a large and prosperous family. She was a middle-aged woman, and being the senior-most wife could only wear the anklet of her husband's titles. And she was always the first to receive the horn of wine from her husband. In fact, women in their maligned femininity, are quite crucial to the development of Achebe's setting of plot and character. As the tribal culture is lost due to the arrival of Europeans, men become fearful women, and women become bold men, leaving their homes and husbands. In TFA, Okonkwo looks back to the "days when men were men" (180). The colonial impact seems to have brought strength and vigour for the women to fight against the oppression of men.

In Igbo society, women were bought and sold into marriage. The bride-price was decided with the help of broomsticks. In the Ibo culture, the bride's dowry consisted of cooking–pots, wooden bowls, brooms, mortar, and pestle, baskets, baskets of cocoyam, and many more products. The woman's condition becomes prominent in the lines quoted by Achebe's character, Ezeulu:

> Different people have different reasons for marrying. Apart from children which we all want, some men want a woman to cook their meals, some want a woman to help on the farm, others want someone they can beat (*Arrow of God* 64).

On special occasions, the women plaited their hair in a new Otimili fashion and decorated their waist with fifteen strings of jigida. They made black patterns on their bodies with the juice of the uli tree. To be a virgin was a big thing in Nigeria, and was considered as a powerful symbol of unity, love, heaven, and beauty. In the Igbo society, the bridegroom gave gifts to his wife's mother if found his wife to be a virgin. Joseph talks of his girlfriend that "...She was a virgin when I met her, which is very rare here" (Achebe, *No Longer at Ease* 17).

In *A Man of the People*, there are images of women playing traditional roles, such as, singers and dancers, or women adoring rich politicians like Chief, the Honourable M.A. Nanga. Achebe shows woman as a mirror reflecting a society that had gone completely rotten and maggoty at the centre. All that was needed was a clean duster to end up the corruption in the society. Mr. Nanga, a corrupt man of 50, plans to marry another girl who is of his daughters' age. This is because "...his missus is too 'bush' for his present position so he wants a bright new 'parlour-wife' to play hostess at his parties"(23). In this novel, Chinua Achebe depicts the insignificant role of women in Igbo society. Mrs. Eleanor John, a tough party woman and board member—rich and independent—is cast as a semi-literate businesswoman with no noteworthy role. Chief Nanga's wife, a beneficiary of the colonial, utilitarian education seems to be helpless on seeing her husband's extramarital relationship and impending marriage to the young Edna. Achebe, no doubt, shows Mrs. Nanga as modern, but then reveals her traditional role. Odili, whom she had asked for help, when tries to unseat her husband, defends her husband, to retain her social and economic position. Consequently, she remains a dependent figure, deriving validity as a human being from her husband. In this novel, Odili's father had five wives and 35 children who married a young girl at the age of 70. Achebe's female characters seem to be mere possessions who added to the glory of men. Edna agrees to marry Chief Nanga as she believed in her destiny and felt that: "If God says that I will be happy in any man's house I will be happy" (Achebe, *A Man of the People* 111).

Clara, in *No Longer at Ease,* is a forbidden woman, an *osu*—descendant of a slave caste. She has been portrayed sympathetically as she breaks her relationship with Obi, for his career as a civil servant.The pregnant Clara gets an abortion and fades out of the story. But Achebe has depicted her as an educated and independent nurse who could do without Obi Okonkwo. Bonnie. J. Barthold in *Black Time Fiction* states that in contrast to Western Fiction, the Forbidden woman in Black Fiction is never forbidden by reason of her virginity. For the most part in black fiction, sexual initation takes place before the story actually begins and the conflict is not about the retention or loss of virginity, but about procreation, child birth, or marriage. According to Barthold, a Forbidden Women is: "Not only is she never a Virgin, neither is she ever a Rebel against her status as a Mule. She plays her part as a catalyst for destruction and either disappears or is herself destroyed"(117). Clara in *No Longer at Ease,* is a Forbidden Women, who is herself destroyed as she suffers from a long illness after having an abortion. The issue of virginity makes the African society quite different from the Indian one. In Indian society, a family stands as an institution to which virginity provides a supporting structure. Moreover, virginity makes the marital relationship sacred and long-lasting.

In *Anthills of the Savannah,* Achebe through his protagonists, Beatrice and Ikem talks about the role of women in Nigerian society. Beatrice blames Ikem for having no clear role for women in his political thinking, and for his inability to understand them. Ikem admits it saying:

> You charged me with assigning to women the role of a fire-brigade after the house has caught fire and been virtually consumed. Your charge has forced me to sit down and contemplate the nature of oppression... (Achebe 88-89).

Achebe's *Girls at War*, shows that the girls and the women took themselves seriously and actively participated in the war. At the road block, Reginald Nwankwo, Ministry of Justice is thoroughly checked by Gladys, a militia girl which astonishes him:

> But after that encounter at the Awka check-point he simply could not sneer at the girls again, nor at the talk of revolution, for he had seen it in action in that young woman whose devotion had simply and without self-righteousness convicted him of gross levity. What were her words? We are doing the work you asked us to do (Achebe 103).

Achebe portrays marriage as more than an affair between two individuals, as a union of two family groups. In *Things Fall Apart*, marriages were contracted after elaborate negotiations and public ceremonies, as is exemplified in the uri ceremony of Akueke, Obierika's daughter. On this occasion, Obierika's family entertains almost the entire village. In every matter, decisions were made by men. It is quite evident by their dominating behaviour in the wife abuse trial conducted by the elders in between Uzowulu and his wife. However Okonkwo, in *Things Fall Apart*, who abuses his wives, has a very endearing relationship with one of them, Ekwefi—his childhood sweetheart. Even true romantic love affairs did exist in between some married couples in this society, as is exemplified by the marital bliss of Ogbuefi Ndulue and his wife, Ozeemena. So strong is their love for one another that the husband never does anything without consulting his wife first.

In *A Man of the People*, Achebe shows that Odili's relationship was never in cordial terms with his father. His father being the local chairman of the People's Organization Party in his village Urua, could not withdraw himself from the sphere of power and authority. He was inwardly pleased with the thought of a "slice of the national cake" which Odili would get in politics:

> The only comment I remember my father making (at the beginning anyway) was when he asked if my "new" party was ready to give me enough money to fight Nanga. He sounded a little doubtful. But he was clearly satisfied with what I had got out of it so far, especially the car which he was now using nearly as much as myself. The normal hostility between us was put away in a corner, out of sight (116).

In Achebe's defence, most critics do find that his novel *Anthills of Savannah* is an attempt to move his female characters from voicelessness to voice. Achebe presents Beatrice Okoh, as a "New Woman of Modern Africa", who is capable of decisive actions. In a male-dominated world, she embodies the spirit of struggle, as her name at baptism, Nwanyibuife—'a female is also something', correctly implies. She warns her fiancée Chris of the danger posed by his passivity and inertness in the affairs of the state, vis-à-vis his association with Sam. Her prophetic warning of the dangers lurking behind all of them is significant. Finally, she is left alone to reconstruct the dehumanized society. She refutes the notion that she needs a man, and slowly learns about Idemili, a goddess balancing the aggression of male power. She even musters up courage to raise the child of Ikem and his mistress, Elewa, who was christened with a boys' name—Amaechina—which literally means "May-the-path-never close". Although at the end of the novel, Beatrice is shown in a nurturing mother-type role, she remains firm in her conviction that women should not be limited to such capacities.

In his novel *A Man of the People,* Achebe presents a strong woman character, Eunice, who is the lawyer and the fiancée of Odili's schoolmate Max. She is the founder of the Common People's Convention that opposes corrupt Chief Nanga and people like him. When Max is shot by thugs of a political adversary, Eunice takes out a pistol and kills Chief Koko. To this strong protrait, Achebe adds pointedly:

> Only then did she fall down on Max's body and begin to weep like a woman; and then the policemen seized her and dragged her away. A very strange girl, people said (144).

Achebe seems to be pragmatic and flexible as he also shows the power and strength of the women in Igbo society. In Achebe's novel *Things Fall Apart,* we observe women performing various roles sprinkled throughout the novel: "The women weeded the farm three times at definite periods in the life of the yams, neither early nor late" (31). This was an extremely important duty, considering that if this task was not carried out correctly, the yam crops would fail. Some chosen women painted the houses of the egwugwu—the clan's ancestral spirits depicting their significance in Ibo society. Achebe also presents women as educators of their children. The women told folk stories to their children to teach them about the human condition and Ibo myths. This facilitated in developing the Ibo culture in the children. Achebe has virtually depicted that in all spheres of life, boys and girls, and men and women, knew what was expected of them. In the family, women swept the house, washed the plates, and cooked the food, while the boys or the men split the firewood, pounded the yam foofoo, and climbed the palm trees. In *Things Fall Apart,* when Okonkwo returns to his mother's clan after being exiled from the Ibo village, Uchendu reproaches Okonkwo for his sorrow about having to come to live with his mother's clan and explains:

> It's true that a child belongs to its father. But when a father beats his child, it seeks sympathy in its mother's hut. A man belongs to his fatherland when things are good and life is sweet. But when there is sorrow and bitterness he finds refuge in his motherland. Your mother is there to protect you. She is buried there. And that is why we say that mother is supreme (122).

In Achebe's works, there is an ontological balance between male and female principles, especially in respect of the major divinities of the land: the goddess of the Earth (Ani) has a male (Ezeani) as chief priest, while the male Oracle of the Hills and the Caves (Agbala) is served by the priestess Chielo. In *Things Fall Apart,* the women routinely perform the role of priestess—the priestess is Chielo—"the priestess of Agbala, the Oracle of the Hill and the Caves" (97). In an episode in the novel, Achebe shows that Chielo comes for Okonkwo's daughter Ezinma. Okonkwo pleads with her to come in the morning as Ezinma was then asleep.

But the priestess screams: "Beware, Okonkwo! Beware of exchanging words with Agbala. Does a man speak when a god speaks? Beware!" (91) Achebe reveals a clear degree of reverence for women in Ibo society. Barthold in *Black Time Fiction* comments:

> Chielo in *Things Fall Apart* exemplifies the spiritual power of the Priestess, a power recognized and honored by the community, sanctified by ritual and invulnerable to the whims of individual men and women (104).

In *Things Fall Apart,* Achebe also unveils woman's power in the representation of the earth goddess, Ani. The Feast of the New Yam was the occasion for giving thanks to Ani. Before the harvest began, it was an Igbo custom to honour the earth goddess by offering the new yams to them. As she was the source of all fertility, without her blessings, crops were not grown:

> Ani played a greater part in the life of the people than any other deity. She was the ultimate judge of morality and conduct. And what was more, she was in close communion with the departed fathers of the clan whose bodies had been committed to earth (33).

Just as Wole Soyinka presents the women characters, which seem to combine the Bitch and the Madonna; Achebe presents some women as embodiment of frailty, whereas some as nurturers of the Ibo people, the caretakers of the yam crops, and the mothers and educators of the Ibo children. Women in *Things Fall Apart,* are insulted and oppressed, but their contribution to farm and family is at some places acknowledged. Achebe refutes the notion that his novels speak against women. He rather says that:

> I want to sort to scream that *Things Fall Apart* is on the side of women...And that Okonkwo is paying the penalty for his treatment of women; that all his problems, all the things he did wrong, can be seen as offenses against the feminine ("Masculinity and Femininity").

Even Soyinka, in his novel *The Interpreters,* shows Dehinwa-the Secretary not as a symbol, but as a member of the new generation.

Soyinka feels that exceptions are always there and the writers cannot enter the mind and the body of a woman. He personally feels that:

> A women's shape, a woman's reproductive capacity which is unique to the female sex just sets her apart from men. It doesnot mean that women are not equal to men intellectually, in capacities and so on and so forth (*Writing Across Worlds* 29).

Wole Soyinka, Toni Morrison, and Richard Wright have reduced women to the means by which a sense of temporal order is achieved to the most immediate cause of time's disruption. In Soyinka's *The Interpreters*, Egbo would bury himself in the breasts of a woman dancer, and thus "seal" himself in time. In Morrison's *The Bluest Eye*, Cholly Breedlove directs his race against the black girl beneath him, when he is interrupted by a pair of white men who shine a flashlight on his naked buttocks, and ordered him to get on with it. He hated the girl as she was the one who had created the situation. In Wright's *Native Son*, Bigger Thomas in his sexual violence against Bessie, finds himself an "anchor in time", but then he bludgeons her to prevent her from betraying him to the police, and to an imprisonment of total dispossession. The three characters Egbo, Cholly Breedlove, and Bigger Thomas reduce the reality of female character to a single dimension—its capacity to help or hinder the masculine struggle against time. The three writers—Soyinka, Morrison and Wright—feel that their characters are the by-products of No Man's Land. Hander in *Chinua Achebe's Biography and Style* mentions that Achebe's African feminine is different from the western female model for a lot of other reasons:

> Achebe seeks to link (...) the question of African women's roles to the larger problems of the post-colonial nation (...). The women, who have simultaneously broken the rules of race and gender, (...) embody hope for the future of the nation. This assertion that women are integral in the building of the new African society emphasizes that damaging effect of oppression outside the colonized-colonizer relationship (...). Achebe goes beyond the notion of conflict to propose that hope lies not in separating women's issues from

society's issues, but in integrating them, and in looking to women continually in the process of social change ("Postcolonial Motherism").

Fig 24. Women empowerment

Source: Electronic.

Achebe does seem to accept that African women are the spiritual base of every family, community, and nation. In *African Short Stories*, Achebe represents women as incarnations of "the last hope for the restoration of the natural order in life and in every sphere of life" ("Postcolonial Motherism").

Elvira Godona, in the article "Postcolonial Motherism", writes that Achebe seems to suggest that the colonized African soil, "has been totally dominated by men, is coloured by wars, civil strife, hunger, famine, tyranny and genocide (...) calls for a return to the mother essence, in other words women and motherist leaders."

Achebe asserts in *Anthills of the Savannah* that he has not created Beatrice, the first major character, out of pressure from the feminists. Rather he admits the presence of Beatrice in all his fictions, from *No Longer at Ease, A Man of the People,* right down to *Anthills of the Savannah.* He says that when the men Struggle, are beaten and cannot defend their rights, then emerges the woman to save them from the humiliation:

> There is a certain increase in the importance I assign to women in getting us out of the mess that we are in, which is a reflection of the role of women in my traditional culture—that they do not interfere in politics until men really make such a mess that the society is unable to go backward or forward. Then women will move in...
>
> ("The Paris Review").

Works Cited

Achebe, Chinua. *A Man of the People.* New York : Anchor, 1966.

______________ *Anthills of the Savannah.* New York : Anchor, 1987.

______________ *Arrow of God.* New York : Anchor,1974.

______________ *Girls at War and Other Stories.* New York : Anchor, 1973.

______________ *No Longer at Ease.* New York: Anchor,1960.

______________ *Things Fall Apart.* New Delhi : Allied, 2004.

Barthold, Bonnie. J. *Black Time Fiction of Africa, The Caribbean and the United States.* New Haven : Conn: Yale Univ. Press, 1981.

Brooks, Jerome. "The Art of Fiction: Chinua Achebe". *The Paris Review.* 1994www. swisseduc.ch/english/reading list/achebe_chinua/ author_by.html_10K.

Brown, Jane Martin. "Water Marks". *Role of Women in Chinua Achebe's Things Fall Apart.* January 2006</theme/1350/women.html>being present</theme/ 1614/ present.html>inIbo society.

Godono, Elvira. "Postcolonial Motherism". 23 Sep 2005 *http:// www.postcolonial* web.org/Africa/godona/.html.

Masculinity and femininity".http://www.123helpme.come/assets/ 14746.html.

Mezu, Rose Ure. "Women in Achebe's World". *WTR* Spring/Summer 1995.

file://c:\Documents%20 and %20 Settings\administrator\ Desktop\Women%20 IN%20 ACHEBE'S%20W...21/2/2005.

Stowe, Harriet Beecher. *Uncle Tom's Cabin.* Kent : Wordworth-editions, 1995.

Wole Soyinka in an interview with Mary David (1985). *Writing Across Worlds: Contemporary Writers talk.* Ed. Susheila Nasta. London: Routledge, 2004.

8 Achebe's Quest from Anarchy to Order

Chinua Achebe presents a true picture of the African social environment along with its cultural past. He brings to the foreground the elements of change, inherent in every human society with its own fallacies and faults. He seems to be somewhat disappointed seeing the 'anarchy' in African society. Achebe agrees with a political scientist who pronounced some years ago: "Nigeria has an Igbo problem and that every ethnic group is of course something of a problem for Nigeria's easy achievement of cohesive nationhood"(Achebe, *The Trouble with Nigeria* 45).

Achebe is unable to understand why for Africa, the sum of evil becomes more than the sum of good. He is astonished at the corruption, gross inequities, noisy vulgarity, and the selfishness of the African society. He feels that the good within them is overpowered by the negative energy within them which instigates them to do evil. He is not hesitant to describe the inherent anarchy or lawlessness in the African society which is due to the European Colonialism..

He describes their struggle and suffering for the independence from the European imperial powers. The aftermath of postindependence era which is full of disillusionment also finds place in the works of Achebe. In his Interview with Cris Searle, Achebe told that Africa's meeting with Europe was devastating. He asserts that African had their own history and culture before arrival of the white. With the coming of Europeans, Africa lost its grip over their history which merely became a foot-note in the history of the alien races in Africa. Achebe expresses that the Africans had virtually forgotten their history as it was not written down.

It cannot be denied that it was 'anarchy' in Africa which inspired Achebe to go into the depth of it to find out the truth. He corelated Africa to the falcon, the bird of prey who could not hear the call of the falconer, that is, the calls of the trainer and so gets brutally killed. It was W.B. Yeats's poem, "The Second Coming" which inspired him to title his most popular novel as *Things Fall Apart*:

> Turning and turning in the widening gyre
> The falcon cannot hear the falconer;
> Things fall apart; the centre cannot hold;
> Mere anarchy is loosed upon the world.
>
> (*The Faber Book of Modern Verse* 58).

Achebe's novel *Things Fall Apart* (TFA), shows the chaos and confusion in Nigerian society due to the colonial impact. It not only tore apart a culture which was truly democratic but also created a new set of attitude towards material possessions. And then there was no turning back for Igbo clan from a confused state. The climax is provided when Umuofia decides to discuss the worsening situation.The existing realities make them acutely aware of the divisions in the Igbo society:

> We who are here this morning have remained true to our fathers, but our brothers have deserted us and joined a stranger to soil their fatherland. If we fight the stranger we shall hit our brothers and perhaps shed the blood of a clansman. But we must do it. Our fathers never dreamt of such a thing, they never killed their brothers. But a white man never came to them. So we must do what our fathers would never have done (Achebe, *TFA* 183).

The policy of British which brought anarchy in Igbo society, is clearly shown in *Arrow of God* (AOG), where the warrant chiefs become notorious for their corruption and exploitation. The Warrant Chief appointed in Okperi by Winter bottom, became little tyrants over their own people. It is quite strange that a man who had got no entity before he was crowned, became so much supportive of the court clerks and messengers, that he forgot his own people, rather became against them. Achebe feels that, "It seems to be a trait in the character of the negro"(108). The bewilderment of the Nigerians with regard to the appointment of warrant chief in Nigeria is reflected in Chinua's novel AOG, when Ezeulu rejects the offer of Clarke:

"Well, are you accepting the offer or not ?" Clarke glowed with the

I-know-this-will-knock-you-over feeling of a benefactor.

"Tell the white man that Ezeulu will not be anybody's chief, except Ulu."

"What!" Shouted Clarke. "Is the fellow mad?"

"I tink so sah," said the interpreter.

"In that case he goes back to prison." Clarke was now really angry. What cheek ! A witch-doctor making a fool of the British Administration in public! (174).

Fig 25. State of lawlessness

Source: Electronic.

Though the Igbos culture and traditions ignored the sensitivity in the human hearts, still Igbos had full faith and respect for their culture. *Things Fall Apart* is a terrible business—as infamous as Clitoridectomy of twins, whom Igbo tradition regards as an abomination [they must be left to die in the bush], and the ritual killing of the boy hostage, Ikemefuna. Okonkwo's great misfortune and exile was the outcome of his killing of a 16-year-old boy of his clan during a sacred ceremony. He had seven wasted and weary years in his motherland Mbanta, where passing each day was painful to him. He lost his place, a chance to lead his warlike clan against the new religion and new culture. Even in Umuofia, the situation had changed due to the influence of the white man. He soon discovers that he is not indispensable for his own clan. Seven years was too long a period to not to expect any change in one's society. Achebe expresses in the novel that a man's place cannot remain the same in his absence. His status, his power, his recognition, everything changes. A man's place is immediately taken by someone else just like the tail of a lizard, if it is lost, another grows up sooner. Thus a man cannot take it for granted his achievements and glories. One has to strive continuously to retain one's position in society.

In *Things Fall Apart* (TFA), Okonkwo's son embraces Christianity not because of his faith in the new religion, but because of his confusion, a sadness which comes from his father's rejection of his abilities and potential. The killing of Ikemefuna by his father reverberates in his heart, and only the poetry of the new religion consoles his heart:

> The hymn about brothers who sat in darkness and in fear seemed to answer a vague and persistent question that haunted his young soul—the question of the twins crying in the bush and the question of Ikemefuna who was killed. He felt a relief within as the hymn poured into his parched soul (Achebe, TFA 134).

In *Things Fall Apart*, Achebe talks of the missionaries who simply walked into the midst of the Igbo tribe with their interpreters, and told them that they worship false gods—gods of woods and stone. The first CMS missionary to the Igbo, the Sierra Leonian, son of Igbo parents, wrote: "May many come willingly to Labour in pulling down the strongholds of Satan's kingdom, for the whole of the Ibo district is his citadel" (qtd. in Isichei, *A History of Christianity* 82). Achebe depicts the power of Christian mission which focused on the breaking down of community norms. In TFA, the evil forest remained no longer evil; the outcasts became no longer outcasts; and the objects and rituals of traditional sacrament were destroyed. The Christian mission aided the colonizing process by pursuing a policy of aggression. Okonkwo's grief was not a personal one, as he mourned for the clan, which he saw breaking up and falling apart. He mourned for the warlike men of Umuofia, who had now become soft like women. In TFA, Okika— a great man and an orator, spoke to Umuofia:

> All our gods are weeping. Idemili is weeping. Ogwugwu is weeping, Agbala is weeping, and all the others. Our dead fathers are weeping because of the shameful sacrilege they are suffering and the abomination we have all seen with our eyes (Achebe 182-183).

In *Arrow of God*, Ezeulu—the Chief Priest of Ulu, symbolically tries to stop time which leads to its disruption, which basically means disaster. He refuses to announce the harvest of 'Yam' which meant famine, as the yams of the previous year could not be disposed off as per the ritual. In the novel, Ezeulu thought himself to be the king of Umuaro who could anticipate the future: "I can see tomorrow; that is why I can tell Umuaro: *come out from this because there is death there or do this because there is profit in it*" (Achebe 132).

Mr. Goodcountry got an opportunity for fruitful intervention, and instead of giving one yam to Ulu, he advised the people to bring it to the church. Three episodes in the narrative, foreshadow Ezeulu's final decision to pit his own vision against the power and welfare of the community: a land dispute with the neighbouring community of Okperi; Oduche's imprisonment of the sacred python; and his own imprisonment by the colonial government. In *Arrow of God*, Ezeulu has a certain awareness of the material consequences. Ezeulu was aware of the consequences, the punishment which Ulu would decide for him. He knew that it was not for now alone but for all time: "It would afflict Umuaro like an *ogulu-aro* disease which counts a year and returns to its victims" (Achebe 220).

In *No longer at Ease,* Chinua shows the impact of corrupt society on every individual. The city of Lagos has been shown as a violent place and like a living thing—like an animal that was going to devour everyone. Even Obi is unable to remain untouched by the changes talking place in Igbo society:

> In Obi's Lagos, the past has taken on the tone of cyclic fatality: Obi, like the *ogbanje* child of *Things Fall Apart,* is caught in a cyclic evil, with little hope of renewing the goodness of time (Barthold, *Black Time Fiction* 91).

Achebe accurately presents the woman's place in African society which is quite inferior to man. A series of births and early deaths of a woman's children, were seen as an embodiment of the malicious spirit known as abiku, ogbanje, dzikwidzikwi, or awomawu—which literally translate as "born-die". He shows Igbo society as largely patriarchal and patrilineal. Families depended on the male offspring for succession and the perpetuation of their names. Achebe also shows the burden on the relationship between fathers and their sons, particularly their first sons. In *Things Fall Apart,* Unoka is the founder of his lineage, but he is not successful in agriculture, the main occupation of his people. He remains busy in merry-making and squandering a lot of money. Even Okonkwo and his son Nwoye's relationship has been shown as quite weak and severed, as the latter develops a craving for exploring the new religion. Achebe depicts the gyres of anarchy in all the spheres of African life. But Achebe's 'Quest for Order' is quiet prominent as he says, "Whatever the strife, the true African spirit never ceases of strife" ("Still hope for Africa"). Achebe's characters seem to reflect the view point of Frantz Fanon who wrote in *Black Skin White Masks*:

> I am black: I am the incarnation of a complete fusion with the world, an intuitive understanding of the earth, an abandonment of my ego in the heart of the cosmos, and no white man, no matter how intelligent he may be, can ever understand Louis Armstrong and the music of the Congo. If I am black, it is not the result of a curse, but it is because, having offered my skin, I have been able to absorb all the cosmic *effluvia.* I am truly a ray of sunlight under the earth...(45).

Achebe feels that it is not only Africa, but every country is struggling against problem—whether its the struggle against famine and hunger, or against corruption. He does not wish to see Africa as a one-issue continent—leadership and apartheid being only one area or issue. Rather Achebe told Chris Searle in *Writing Across Worlds* that:

> In Nigeria we do not have apartheid but the fact that the South African people are locked in this struggle diminishes us and our potential for solving problems in Nigeria. For ultimately it is a struggle about the great wealth of South Africa and its economy and the way this wealth is not used for the benefit of Africa and its people (65).

Achebe achieves a balance in showing the consequences of the clash of two cultures. He is not completely negative when discussing imperialism. Rather he feels that there is a need to get away from pessimism instead of harping on the failure. He also realizes that they must concentrate intelligently upon the examples and signs that have been positive and successful. He believes that colonialism united people by giving them a common language. The Ibo society that Achebe portrays is keenly aware of its history and the accomplishments of their founding fathers. He shows a society where a man is judged not by the size of his inheritance, but by his own personal accomplishments. Moreover, the marital amity and social problems are resolved on the basis of the consensus formed from the open public debate that protects the rights of the individuals, as well as the corporate interests of the community.

Okonkwo of *Things Fall Apart* passes through many of the same stages that Man goes through in the Bible. He rebels against the Father, is forced to earn a living by main labour, is exiled, and finally ends his life in a faux crucifixion. Presumably, Achebe is making the point that those who adhere to the ancient gods and old traditions, those who lead their lives in the grip of fear, must clear out of the way to make room for the coming of a new God and a new Way: "What falls apart is not Umuofia society and culture—which have always survived by adjusting to ever-changing conditions—but Okonkwo, with his selfish goals of greatness" (Ed. Okpewho, *A CaseBook* 40).

Thingnam Kishan Singh, a critique of the novels of Chinua Achebe feels that: "Okonkwo's act can be seen as heroic and worthy of a leader's sacrifice when juxtaposed to the community's passive and inert acceptance of colonial domination" (*Rethinking Colonialism* 68). If Achebe's assessment is true, then:

> *Arrow of God* is doubly a product of the times: first, of the period when Ibo society underwent the radical changes that accompanied the intrusion of British colonialism and Christianity; and second, of the period—in retrospect, a brief moment of the early sixties—when the hope was extended that men of good will, having learned from the past, might restore a new sense of order and social unity (Barthold, *Black Time Fiction* 140).

In Contemporary Writers talk in *Writing Across Worlds*, Wole Soyinka admits that even if one renounces a particular religion, one can learn from that religion, and attain aesthetic delight out of it. Though he renounces Christianity, he has appreciation for the architecture of a church, or a Christian tale, or a Christian symbol. He wants the people to realize that the dates, the rituals, and the crucifixion in Christian religion are all symbols of renewal and that Christianity itself is based on pagan religions. Achebe, no doubt, shows the inequality of the sexes, but does not seem to make them the subject of mild amusement. Nonetheless, he assigns important roles to women. The women painted the houses of egwugwu, the spiritual power. Furthermore, the first wife of a man in the Ibo society is paid some respect. In *Things Fall Apart,* this deference is illustrated by the palm wine ceremony at Nwakibie's *Obi*—house, when Anasi—Nwakibie's first wife, had not arrived and "others[other wives] could not drink before her, and so they stood waiting" (Achebe 18). Achebe has come up with the most positive female archetype. In *Anthills of Savannah,* Beatrice is compared with Idemili, an African mythical goddess. Achebe's Idemili actually means the pillar of war and the source of Edimili River is a lake. It runs through the territory throughout which the python is held sacred. Chielo in *Things Fall Apart* exemplifies the spiritual power of the Priestess, who was honoured by the Igbo society, and was invulnerable to the whims of individual men and women. According to Barthold:

> In traditional Africa, women were the biological embodiment of the mythic cycle, by virtue of procreation and childbirth. But they were often spiritual leaders, priestesses, as well, charged along with their male counterparts with nurturing the mythic cycle through appropriate rituals and sacrifice (*Black Time Fiction* 100).

In Achebe's novels, the 'Ancestral spirits' were the intermediaries between the material and the spiritual world. They protected the present and guaranteed the future, free of doubts and worries. Achebe shows full allegiance to his past culture, but is also willing to accept the new culture and religion. Barthold in *Black Time Fiction* (BTF) expresses that:

> The balance that has been achieved between traditional African culture and western influence reflects an essential facet of African culture: its well-documented capacity to absorb foreign influence into existing institutions (20).

Achebe feels that Igbos are not just static subjects of the changes happening around them, but participate actively in the changes taking place in their conceptual universe. He is of the opinion that the Igbos chose Christianity, as Nwoye did; or rejected it, as Okonkwo did, because they were aware of themselves making their own world in time. Even though the characters in Achebe's novels fail to attain their aspirations due to the intrusion of colonialism and Christianity, but the clan, the social group remains intact:

> African novels are "novels of situation" rather than "novels of character," that the community of "Umuofia, not Okonkwo, becomes the main character of *Things Fall Apart*". James Olney goes even further, insisting that "the character in African fiction *typifies* the family, the extended family, the clan, the culture; only incidentally is he himself " (qtd. in BTF 83).

Achebe has presented a critical picture of the African past, without idealizing and glorifying a society which suffered immensely through the ravages of time. He has proved that unless a race uses its own talents, takes pride in its own history, and loves its own memories, it can never fulfil itself completely, Okey Ndibe feels:

> Big African laughter can only come from a people who have suffered (and survived) enslavement, colonial bondage, neo-colonial subjugation, famine, internal repression, and civil wars ("Still Hope for Africa").

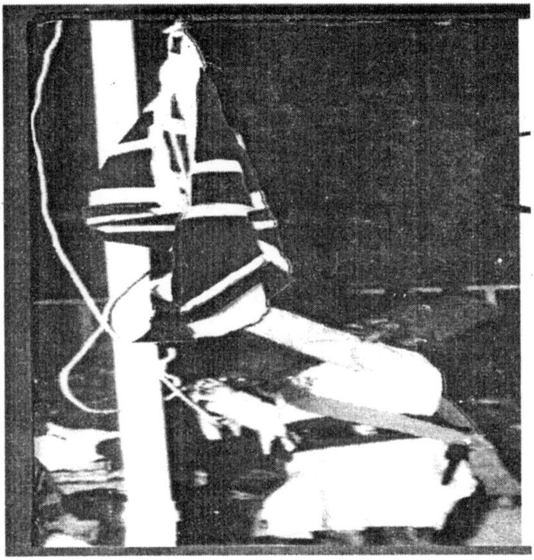

Fig 26. Trevor Royle, *Winds of Change: The End of Empire in Africa* (Great Britain: John Murray, 1996). N.Pag.

Achebe is of the opinion that the new culture and tradition should not be imposed upon the individuals, but should be left on them to decide upon. Achebe feels that they have seen lots of problems in the past, and they are older than these problems. Just as the masquerade in Igbo festivals, that dances and moves through the big arena, Achebe feels that a writer has to keep moving and tell the stories from different perspectives. Achebe feels that:

> Our problems have been there for hundreds of years and they vary from place to place, country to country. So we must be prepared to face this complexity, as untidy as it may seem, because this is the only way we shall make progress (*Writing Across Worlds* 62).

Wole Soyinka, the Nobel Laureate for Literature, in his book *The Burden of Memory, the Muse of Forgiveness*, challenges the notion of simple forgiveness, of confession and absolution, as strategies for social healing. Like Achebe, Soyinka also feels that it is because of the cocky leaders and cheerleaders that a country is divided. In his book, Soyinka says that, "the division of India and Pakistan (and the allocation of their respective boundaries) owed to the whimsical decisions of a mere civil servant imported straight from Whitehall, someone who had never even visited the Asian continent until then..." (*The Burden of Memory* 40-41). Soyinka ridicules that may be the same civil servant would be invited to sort out the mess of African boundaries that enclose them today. Achebe's acceptance of the truth about Africa has fetched the Africans rewards.

On 5 November 2008, Barack Obama, a young African-American law-maker from Illinois became the 'First Black President' of America—the most powerful country in the world. The change has come not only for Americans, but also for the Africans. Obama's victory is the victory of Africans, who have been struggling for years. Kenyans in Barack Obama's ancestral homeland, sang and danced with joy as the Illinois Senator they saw as one of their own become the U.S. President. This has made the Africans feel pride in their traditional culture and traditions.

The 'Dreams' of Chinua Achebe and other African Writers will not take much time to get fulfilled, their Quest from 'Anarchy' to 'Order' will be achieved. Achebe is sanguine about the creation of Nigerian nations as he says that, "And I just hope, as nothing goes on forever, that we will find a way to stumble out of this anarchy" ("The Paris Review").

Works Cited

Achebe, Chinua. *Arrow of God*. New York : Anchor, 1974.

______________ *The Trouble with Nigeria*. London: Heinemann, 1983.

______________ *Things Fall Apart*. New Delhi : Allied, 2004.

Barthold, Bonnie. J. *Black Time Fiction of Africa, The Caribbean and the United States*. New Haven: Conn:. Yale Univ. Press, 1981.

Chinua, Achebes Things Fall Apart: A Case Book. Ed. Isidore Okpewho. New York: Oxford University, 2003.

Fanon, Frantz. *Black Skin White Masks*. New York : Grove, 1967.

Isichei, Elizabeth. *A History of Christianity in Africa : From Antiquity to the Present*. London : Cromwell, 1995.

James Olney, *Tell Me Africa.*

Ndibe, Okey. "Still Hope for Africa". *A Viewpoint*. 24 May 2000 http :/ /news.bbc.co.uk/1/hi/world/africa/760924.stm.

Singh, Thingnam Kishan. *Rethinking Colonialism : A Critique of the novels of Chinua Achebe and Ngũgĩ wa Thiong'o*. Delhi: Worldview, 2006.

Soyinka, Wole. *The Burden of Memory, the Muse of Forgiveness*. New York: OxfordUniversity Press, 1999.

"The Art of Fiction: Chinua Achebe". *The Paris Review*. 2007 *www.swisseduc.ch/english/reading* list/achebe-chinua/author-by.html-10k_.

The Faber Book of Modern Verse. "The Second Coming." Ed. Michael Roberts. Rev.Donald Hall.3rd ed. London : Faber and Faber Limited, 1965.

Writing Across Worlds: Contemporary Writers talk. Ed. Susheila Nasta. London: Routledge, 2004.

Bibliography

A. Primary Sources

Fiction

Achebe, Chinua. *A Man of the People*. New York: Anchor, 1966.

______________ , *Anthills of the Savannah*.New York: Anchor, 1987.

______________ , *Arrow of God*. New York: Anchor, 1974.

______________ *No Longer at Ease*, New York: Anchor, 1960.

______________ , *Things Fall Apart*. New Delhi: Allied, 2004.

Non-Fiction

Achebe, Chinua. *Girls at War and other Stories*. New York: Anchor, 1973.

______________ , *Home and Exile*. New York: Anchor, 2000.

______________ , *Hopes and Impediments: Selected Essays*. New York : Anchor, 1988.

______________ , *The Trouble with Nigeria*. London: Heinemann, 1983.

B. Secondary Sources

Ashcraft, Bill, Griffiths Gareth, and Tiffin Helen. The *Empire Writes Back*. 2nd ed. London: Routledge, 2002.

Awoonor, Kofi. *The Breast of the Earth: A Survey of the History, Culture, Literature of Africa South of the Sahara*. Doubleday, 1976.

Barthold, Bonnie. J. *Black Time Fiction of Africa, The Caribbean and the United States*. New Haven: Conn: Yale Univ. Press, 1981.

Blake, Robert. A *History of Rhodesia*. 1st ed. New York: Knopf, 1977.

Boahen, A. Adu. *African Perspectives on Colonialism*. Baltimore: Johns Hopkins University Press, 1989.

Boyce, Davies, Carole. *Black Women, Writing and Identity: Migrations of the Subject*. New York: Routledge, 1994.

Carroll, David. *Chinua Achebe*. 2nd ed. New York: St. Martin's Press, 1980.

Chinua Achebe's Things Fall Apart: A CaseBook. Ed. Isidore Okpewho. New York: Oxford University, 2003.

Coetzee, J.M. *White Writing : On the culture of Letters in South Africa*. New Haven: Yale University Press, 1988.

Diop, Cheikh Anta. *The Cultural Unity of Black Africa: The Domains of Patriarchy and of Matriarchy in Classical Antiquity*. Chicago, IL: Third World Press, 1990.

Killam, G.D. *The Writing of East and Central Africa*. Portsmouth, NH: Heinemann, 1985.

Fanon, Frantz. *Black Skin White Masks*. New York: Grove, 1967.

February, V.A. *Mind Your Colour: The 'coloured' stereotype in South African Literature* London: Kegan Paul, 1981.

Gathering Seaweed: African Prison Writing. Ed. Jack Mapanje. London:Heinemann, 2002.

Gikandi, Simon. *Reading Chinua Achebe: Language and Idcology in Fiction*. London: James Currey, 1991.

Isichei, Elizabeth. *A History of Christianity in Africa: From Antiquity to the present*. London: Cromwell, 1995.

Larson, Charles. *The Emergence of Africa Fiction*. London: Macmillan, 1978.

Lindfors, Bernth. *Folklore in Nigerian Literature*. New York: Africana Publishing, 1973.

Majumdar, Bimalendu. *Joyce Cary: An Existentialist Approach*. New Delhi: Associated, 1982.

Mazrui, Ali. *The Africans : A Triple Heritage*. Canada: Little, Brown, 1986.

Mehta, Gurleena and Narang Harish. *Apartheid in Fiction*. New Delhi: Commonwealth, 1990.

Mudimbe, V.Y. *The Innention of Africa*. Bloomington : Indiana UP, 1988.

Ngara Emmunuel. *Stylistic Criticism and African Novel*. London: Heinemann, 1982.

Palmer, Eustace. *The Growth of the African Novel*. London: Heinemann, 1979.

Rogozinski, Jan. *A Brief History of the Caribbean: From the Arawak and the Carib to the Present*. New York: Meridian-Penguin, 1994.

Royle, Trevor. *Winds of Change: The End of Empire in Africa*. London: John Murray, 1996.

Singh, Thingnam Kishan. *Rethinking Colonialism : A Critique of the novels of Chinua Achebe and Ngugi wa Thiong'o*. Delhi: Worldview, 2006.

Soyinka Wole. *The Burden of Memory, the Muse of Forgiveness*. New York: Oxford University Press, 1999.

Stowe, Harriet Beecher. *Uncle Tom's Cabin*. Kent: Wordworth-editions, 1995.

Sweetman, David. *Women Leaders in African History*. USA: Heinemann, 1984.

The Faber Book of Modern Verse. "The Second Coming". Ed. Michael Roberts. Rev. Donald Hall. 3rd ed. London: Faber and Faber Limited, 1965.

______________, Journey of the Magi. London: Faber and Faber Limited, 1965.

Thiong'o, Ngugi wa. *Decolonising the Mind: The Politics of Language in African Literature.* Delhi: Worldview, 1986.

Writing Across Worlds: Contemporary Writers talk. Ed. Susheila Nasta. London: Routledge, 2004.

C. Articles

Agatucci, Cora. "Chinua Achebe in his own words." *Value and Functions of Literature and Story-telling* (2005).

Akwani, Obi.O. "Chinua Achebe's Things Fall Apart." *Okonkwo: A Life of Fear; a life of Bravery* (2007).

Feldman, Gayle. "Destroying the Horrors of 500 Years." *Black History* Weekly (2000).

Hander, Margaret. "Political Discourse: Theories of Colonialism and Post-Colonialism." *The Term Postcolonial applied to Anthills of the Savannah and A Forest of Flowers* 27 (1997).

Mezu, Rose Ure. "Women in Achebe's World." *Feminism, Womanism and Modern African Women* WTR Spring/Summer (1995) :4-6.

Phillips, Caryl. "Out of Africa." *A Discussion* (2003).

Poff, G. Elissa. "Setting and Context in Works by Achebe, Saro-Wiwa, Ayoda, and Emecheta." *Post imperial and Postcolonial Literature in English* 27 (1999).

Proyect, Louis. "Achebe's Anthills of the Savannah." *Book Review* (1987): 1-5.

Smith, Jason M. "Freudian Psychology in Anthills." *Freud's Id, Ego and Superego in Anthills of the Savannah* 32 (1994): 1-2.

Tahbildar, Barnali. "The Role of the Nigerian Woman." *Emecheta's the Slave Girl* 27 (1997).

D. Electronic Sources

Agatucci, Cora. "African Storytelling." *Article.* 2005 *http://web.cocc.edu/cagatucci/ classes/* hum211/afrstory.htm.

"Anthills of the Savannah." *Review.* 1987 *http:// www.fictionaward winners.com/ reviews.cfm?id* = 45.

Bacon, Katie. "An African Voice." [Interview with Chinua Achebe] *Interviews.*

Atlantic Unbound. 2000 http ://www. theatlantic.com/unbound/ interviews/ba 2000-08-02.htm.

Brown, Jane Martin. "Water Marks". *Role of Women in Chinua Achebe's Things*

Fall Apart. January 2006</theme/1350/women.html>being present</ theme/ 1614/ present.html>inIbo society.

Brooks, Jerome. *"The Art of Fiction."* [Interview with Chinua Achebe.] *The Paris*

Review. 1994 *www.swisseduc.ch/english/reading* list/achebe_chinua/ author_by.html-10k_.

"Chinua Achebe's Things Fall Apart." *Review*. 2005 *file://\\1490006f-4\D\ BrothersJudd_com%20-%* Review %20of % 20 Chinua % 20 Achebe's: ... .

Clarke, John Henrik. "Why Africana History ?" *Race and History*. January 1987 http :// www.raceandhistory.com/historicalviews/2004/ clarke22.html.

Culross, Melissa. "Chinua Achebe and Things Fall Apart." *Review*. 2005 file ://c:\

Documents%20and%20settings\Administrator\Desktop\Chinua%20 Achebe %20&%...

"Embodiment in African Literature." *English Essays*. 2004 http : // www. englishessays. org.uk/english_essays/embodiment_african_ literature.php.

Ezenwo, Ohaeto. *Chinua Achebe: A Biography*. "Igbo people: Clothing and Cosmetic Makeup (at the Time of Things Fall Apart)." 28 Nov 1997 *http://www.africanews.org/west/nigeria/stories/19971128_feat1. html.*

The Igbo People. Ed. Ukwu, Dele Chinwe. January 2000 http: /culture.

Chiamaka.com/Igboclothing.html.

Kawu-Bala, Attahiru. "Black History." *Destroying the Horrors of 500 years – A Review of 500 years later*. 30 March 2007 http: //www. itzcaribbean. com/ 500_years_later.php.

Landow, George. "Post Imperial and Post Colonial Literature in English." *Chinua Achebe: overview*. February 2002 http: // www.scholars.nus. edu.sg/ Landow/post/achebe/achebeov.html.

"Literary giant Chinua Achebe returns "home" from U.S., to love and adulation of community." *A Biography*. 2005 *file:// c:\Documents%20and* %20 Settings \administrator\Desktop\ USAfricaonline%20%20 Literature.htm.

Mezu, Rose Ure. *"Women in Achebe's World"*. WTR Spring/Summer 1995 *file:// c:\Documents%20* and %20 Settings\administrator\ Desktop\ Women%20 IN%20 ACHEBE'S%20W...21/2/2005.

Ndibe, Okey. *Viewpoint : "Still Hope for Africa"*. 24 May 2000 http :// news.bbc.co. uk/1/hi/world/Africa/760924.stm.

"The Brutality of Gender Conflict in Things Fall Apart." *Gender Awareness in Things Fall Apart*. 2006<*http://en.wikipedia.org/wiki/Things Fall Apart*>.

"The Role of Women in Chinua Achebe's Things Fall Apart." *Discerning Truth from Perception*. June 2006 women</theme/1350/ women.html>.

Ukwu, Dele Chinwe. "My Memories of The Nigerian-Biafran Civil War." *Anecdote*. 2000 *culture@Chiamaka.com*.

______________, "The Igbo people." *Origins and History*. 2000 http: // www. qub. ac. uk/ english / imperial/Nigeria/origins.htm.

______________, "The Igbo People." *Language and Culture*. 2000 http : /culture. Chiamaka. com/igbopeople.html.

Index